BEYOND
BASICS

A Developmental Reading Program

GRADE FIVE

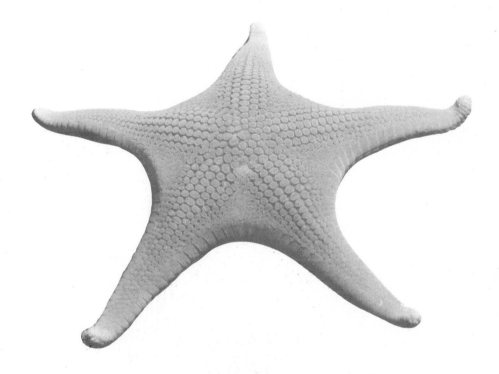

Jamestown Publishers
Providence, Rhode Island

BEYOND BASICS
A Developmental Reading Program
Grade Five

Catalog No. 332

Copyright © 1987 by Jamestown Publishers, Inc.

Developed by B&W Associates, Newport, Rhode Island

Cover and Text design by Deborah Christie

Original Illustrations

Richard Bishop: pp. 12–13, 21, 28–29, 36–37,
   44–45
Robert Brun: pp. 124, 126
Pamela R. Levy: pp. 164–165, 172–173, 175,
   180–181
Thomas Ewing Malloy: pp. 60, 94, 95, 97,
   98, 105, 108–109, 116, 118, 121, 124, 127,
   129–132, 149, 188, 189
Eliza Wells Smith: p. 69
Thom Valentino: p. 124

Printed in the United States MU

87 88 89 90 91 9 8 7 6 5 4 3 2 1

ISBN: 0-89061-430-X

Contents

Developing Literary Skills

I. Main Idea

A. Underline the sentence that tells what the paragraph is about.

Some mountains are born as volcanoes. Mt. Fuji in Japan is one of these. Other mountains are pushed upward by the strong movement of one of the layers under the earth's crust. They are called folded mountains. A third type of mountain is known as a block mountain. And the last type of mountain is called a dome mountain. These are the four main types of mountains found on earth.

B. Draw a line under the one sentence that does *not* belong in the paragraph.

As you might expect, different parts of the world have different types of weather. Most people like to live where there is a mix of hot, cold, rainy and sunny weather. At the North and South Poles, the weather is always cold. At the equator, the weather is always hot. Between those two extremes, weather ranges from wet to dry and from warm to cool.

II. Sequence

Write *1* before the sentence that tells what to do first. Write *2* before the sentence that tells what to do next. Continue numbering the sentences until the sequence is finished.

How to Make Your Own Eyeglass Lens

.... Fill the eyedropper from the glass of water.
.... Draw the water back into the eyedropper. Notice what happens to the *O* as the water is taken away.
.... Spread some butter or margarine around a capital letter *O* on the newspaper page.
.... Put a single drop of water on the letter *O* and compare its size with another capital *O*. Which *O* is larger?
.... Gather a newspaper page, a small bit of butter or margarine, an eyedropper and a glass of water.

III. Cause and Effect

Put a check mark (✔) in front of each sentence that has a cause-and-effect relationship. For each sentence you check, draw one line under the cause and two lines under the effect. (Hint: not every sentence will have a cause-and-effect relationship.)

.... 1. When Lois got over her cold, she returned to school.

.... 2. Moving air masses cause the winds to blow.

.... 3. A black cat crossed in front of Peter, who failed his social studies test later that day.

.... 4. Eloise paid a fine when she returned the overdue library book.

.... 5. Jane hit the nail on its head with a hammer to drive it into the board.

.... 6. You can always tell police officers by the blue uniforms they wear.

IV. Fact and Opinion

Write *F* in front of every sentence that states a fact. Write *O* in front of every sentence that expresses what someone thinks.

.... 1. Many people believe that the Vikings came to America before Christopher Columbus did.

.... 2. The ancient Incas, who lived in South America, were a smarter people than the Aztecs of Mexico.

.... 3. There are many different ways of making sculptures.

.... 4. Unlike oil and watercolor paintings, photographs are not really art.

.... 5. The Antarctic region is one of the coldest places on earth.

V. Drawing Conclusions

Read the paragraph below carefully. Then put an **X** in the box beside the answer that best completes each statement that follows.

> It was a dark night in autumn. The old banker was walking nervously back and forth in his room. He was thinking back to a night in his youth. He recalled every person, every face. He could even hear again what they had talked about. Yes, he remembered every word as if it had been spoken only yesterday.

1. The banker was thinking about something that happened
   - ☐ a. years earlier.
   - ☐ b. just yesterday.
   - ☐ c. at some unknown time.

2. Whatever it was that happened, the banker
   - ☐ a. is amused at the events.
   - ☐ b. quickly turns his thoughts to something else.
   - ☐ c. thinks the events were important.

3. The expression "the old banker was walking nervously" shows that he is
   - ☐ a. waiting for someone to call on him.
   - ☐ b. very smart.
   - ☐ c. still upset by something that happened years ago.

VI. Reference Skills

Put an **X** in the box beside the answer that best completes each statement.

1. A periodical is
   - ☐ a. a magazine or newspaper.
   - ☐ b. another name for a novel.
   - ☐ c. a space of time somewhat shorter than a month.

2. The *Readers' Guide to Periodical Literature* lists
   - ☐ a. the titles of newspaper articles.
   - ☐ b. the titles and dates of magazine articles.
   - ☐ c. places where you can find maps.

3. You are most likely to find a pronunciation key in
   - ☐ a. an almanac.
   - ☐ b. a dictionary.
   - ☐ c. an atlas.

4. A book of maps is called an
   - ☐ a. encyclopedia.
   - ☐ b. atlas.
   - ☐ c. almanac.

5. The best place to look for up-to-date information on the population of a state or a country is an
   - ☐ a. encyclopedia.
   - ☐ b. atlas.
   - ☐ c. almanac.

VII. Textbook Skills

Put an X in the box beside the answer that best completes each statement.

1. A globe is
   - ☐ a. a collection of maps.
   - ☐ b. a special kind of textbook.
   - ☐ c. a scaled-down model of the earth.

2. Special features of most textbooks include
   - ☐ a. illustrations.
   - ☐ b. stories.
   - ☐ c. a foreign language dictionary.

3. To find the pages on which information on a specific topic can be found in a textbook, you should look first in the
   - ☐ a. contents page.
   - ☐ b. bibliography.
   - ☐ c. index.

4. A glossary provides a
   - ☐ a. list of maps.
   - ☐ b. list of specialized words and their meanings.
   - ☐ c. list of other textbooks on the same subject.

5. One reason math textbooks are hard to read is that
   - ☐ a. math has a special language of its own.
   - ☐ b. nobody likes math.
   - ☐ c. writers of these books like to be tricky.

VIII. Literary Skills

Put an **X** in the box beside each answer that best completes the statement.

1. Fiction books
   - ☐ a. are books that tell of real people and real events.
   - ☐ b. tell of imaginary people and events.
   - ☐ c. are the best kind of books to read.

2. Nonfiction books are
   - ☐ a. easier to read than fiction books.
   - ☐ b. more popular than fiction books.
   - ☐ c. any books that are not fiction.

3. A character can be
   - ☐ a. a person in a fiction book.
   - ☐ b. anyone in a biography.
   - ☐ c. a person, animal or thing in a fiction book.

4. The setting of a story is
   - ☐ a. when and where the events take place.
   - ☐ b. who the characters are.
   - ☐ c. how the story will end.

5. Rhyme and rhythm are more likely to be found in
   - ☐ a. fiction books.
   - ☐ b. biographies.
   - ☐ c. poems.

Developing Comprehension Skills

Recognizing the Main Idea

In a good paragraph, all of the sentences work together to develop a main idea.

Read the paragraphs below. Which is a better paragraph?

A tribe of people called Bedouins (BED-o-wins) live in Arabia. There are three deserts there. Oil is pumped on the east coast. The temperature often reaches 120 degrees.

Since the Bedouin people move a lot, they live in tents. The tents can be set up and taken down swiftly. They are woven of goat hair and sheep wool and are supported by stakes driven into the ground. They are braced by ropes. The sides of the tents are lifted or lowered, depending on the weather.

The first paragraph is poorly written. Each sentence brings up a new topic. The second paragraph is a good paragraph. All of the sentences give information about the main idea. Can you tell what that main idea is? Write your answer on the blank line.

If you wrote *Bedouins live in tents,* you are correct. That is the main idea of the paragraph.

Now read the paragraphs below. Underline the one sentence in each paragraph that states the main idea. Check your answers against the key on page 203.

1. The cobra is a poisonous snake. It injects venom into its victim with its fangs. Its victims include animals such as rodents, frogs and toads.

2. Astronomers have discovered thousands of asteroids, or small planets, in space. The smallest are ten to one hundred feet across. The largest asteroids measure five hundred miles!

Main Idea and Detail Sentences

Paragraphs often have two kinds of sentences. One is a **topic sentence**. It tells what the whole paragraph is about. Other sentences are more specific. They give details that tell about the main idea.

Read the paragraph below. Which sentence is the topic sentence? Which sentences give details?

All insects are alike in some ways. An insect's body has three parts. Insects always have six legs.

The first sentence is a general statement about insects. It is the topic sentence. The other two sentences give details about insects.

Underline the topic sentence in the following paragraph. Then write the main idea of the paragraph on the blank line.

It was a beautiful night. The stars glittered brightly against the black sky. The moon was white and full. And the air was a perfect temperature.

The main idea of the paragraph is:

....

Did you underline the first sentence? It states the main idea of the paragraph—*It was a beautiful night.* The other sentences give details about the night. They are too specific to be topic sentences.

A Read each group of sentences below. In each, underline the sentence that states the main idea.

1. Science fiction stories are often set in the future.

    Many science fiction stories also take place on other planets.

    That is why time machines are a popular device in science fiction.

    H.G. Wells was one of the first science fiction writers.

2. Arabic is the main language in North Africa.

    People in East Africa speak Swahili.

    There are more than one thousand languages in Africa.

    English is spoken in South Africa.

3. There are many ways of making sculptures.

    Sculptures can be modeled from soft material such as clay.

    Carving wood and stone is a popular method of sculpture.

    Some sculptures are made from metal.

4. All of the actors created characters that seemed real.

    I especially liked the lead character.

    The movie was exciting from start to finish.

    It was the best movie I've ever seen.

▶

5. The simplest sort of bridge is made from logs.

   The Romans used arches to support their bridges.

   Bridges are platforms that carry traffic across rivers and valleys.

   The first bridges were probably tree trunks.

[B] Write a paragraph about one of your school subjects. First write a topic sentence. Then write two or three detail sentences.

....

....

....

....

....

....

....

Unity in Paragraphs

As you know, a good paragraph has one main idea. All the sentences should work together to support that idea. That gives a paragraph unity.

Does this paragraph have unity?

> Many people think the old house is haunted. My friend Carl says he heard strange noises in the house. Aunt Helen says she saw a ghost.

The topic sentence states what the paragraph is about—a haunted house. The other sentences give details about the subject. All the sentences work together to give the paragraph unity.

Sometimes paragraphs do not have unity. They have sentences that give information that is not related to the main idea. Such paragraphs are weak.

Find and underline the main idea in the paragraph below. Remember that a topic sentence tells the main idea of a paragraph. Then put two lines under the two sentences that do not belong.

> The Age of Reptiles was a period in the earth's history. It began 200 million years ago and lasted 140 million years. Scientists say that the earth is over 4 billion years old. During that time dinosaurs roamed the world. Dinosaur bones are found over much of the world.

Did you pick the first sentence as the topic sentence? It tells you that the paragraph is about the Age of Reptiles. That is the main idea.

Did you put two lines under sentences 3 and 5? They do not support the main idea. One tells about the age of the earth. The other tells where dinosaur bones are found. The other sentences in the paragraph give details about the Age of Reptiles.

▶

Write three details about the Age of Reptiles on the blank lines.

1. ....

....

2. ....

....

3. ....

....

☐ The paragraphs below lack unity. Each contains one sentence that does not support the main idea. On the blank line after each paragraph, write the main idea. Then underline the sentence that does not support it.

Photography is a wonderful hobby. Everyone should have a hobby. Anyone can learn to take good pictures. All you need is the right camera and some practice.

The main idea is ....

....

It had been a long, hard winter for the Joelsons. Several heavy storms had kept the family snowed in for weeks. They almost ran out of food. There are five people in the Joelson family.

The main idea is ....

....

Lions live in family groups called prides. A pride may have five or six females, a male or two, and several young. Other jungle animals live alone. Each pride has its own hunting area.

The main idea is ....

The people in our building have some unusual pets. Mr. Conroy has a skunk. The Vielas keep three rabbits. Not all animals make good pets. My friend Karen has a pet grasshopper.

The main idea is ....

Syd was never on time. He would try, but something always got in the way. The phone would ring. He would oversleep. His watch would stop. Syd worked in a candy store.

The main idea is .... ■

Understanding Sequence

One way to tell a story is to describe events in the order in which they happened. The first event is described first, the second event next, and so on. This is called **time-sequence order**.

The sentences below describe a series of events. Are the events arranged in time-sequence order?

1. The player came up to bat.
2. The ball sailed over the fence and out of the ballpark.
3. On the third pitch, he connected solidly with the ball.
4. He swung and missed the first pitch.
5. Then he hit a foul tip.

Obviously, the order of events makes no sense. For example, the batter could not hit a foul tip after he hit the ball over the fence. Read the sentences again. Pay attention to words such as *first, then* and *third*. They are clues to the order of events.

Now look at the sentences below, in their proper order:

1. The player came up to bat.
2. He swung and missed the first pitch.
3. Then he hit a foul tip.
4. On the third pitch, he connected solidly with the ball.
5. The ball sailed over the fence and out of the ballpark.

The sentences make a lot more sense that way, don't they?

Read the sentences below. Then number the events from 1 to 5 in time sequence. Check your answers against the answer key on page 203.

.... Then she went to math, her first class of the day.

.... When the bell rang at 12:15, it was time for lunch.

.... Carla went to her locker as soon as she got to school.

.... Carla was almost late for science, her second class.

.... Carla had three afternoon classes before she went home.

LET'S SEE, THAT WAS H_2O FIRST, THEN NITRIC ACID, THEN CHLORINE AND FINALLY COPPER SULFATE — OR WAS IT NITRIC ACID FIRST, THEN H_2O ... OR ....

Understanding Time-Signal Words

Look at the following words. In what way are they alike?

before	finally	while
after	then	when

All of the words have to do with time. When they are used in sentences, these words signal when something happened.

For instance, the word *before* tells that one action or event happened at an earlier time than another, as in this sentence:

Juanita raised her hand before she went to the board.

What does the word *after* signal in the following sentence?

After he got home, Michael went to his room
to study.

The word *after* signals an event that happened later than something else. In this case, Michael arrived home. After that he went to his room.

Two other words—*then* and *finally*—tell that something happened after something else. *Then* is used to mean "next," and *finally* means "last." Use each of the words in a sentence to show that Michael went to his room after he got home.

....

....

....

....

....

....

Now read the following sentence. Can you tell which event happened first?

I saw a rainbow while it was raining.

The word *while* signals that the two events happened at the same time. If you substitute the word *when* in the sentence, you will see that the meaning is unchanged. Both *while* and *when* signal events that happened at the same time.

Here are some other time-signal words you may come across in your reading:

first	now	earlier
second	later	afterward
last	next	once

Use them to help you determine the order of events in the things you read.

☐ Underline the time-signal words in the following pairs of sentences. Then answer the questions that follow each pair.

1. First the roof fell in. Then the house collapsed.

   Which event happened first? ....

2. Jack listened to the radio while he ate his lunch. After lunch, he went back to work.

   Which event happened last? ....

   ....

   Which two events happened at the same time? ....

   .... ▶

3. When the speaker started, the people in the crowd were quiet. After the speech ended they cheered.

Which event happened last? ....

....

Which two events happened at the same time?

....

....

4. I planted three trees before the storm. Afterward, I found that two had been knocked over.

Which event happened first? ....

When did the storm come? ....

....

After what event were the trees found knocked over?

....

5. After John bought a new pair of skates, he practiced every day. Now he is the best skater on the team.

Which event happened first? ....

....

When did John practice every day? ....

....

When did he become the best skater? ....

....

Arranging Events in Time Sequence

In writing, events are not always arranged in time-sequence order. You need to pay attention to signal words to help you determine when things happened.

Read the sentence below. Circle the event that happened first.

The dog barked after he saw the cat.

Did you circle the second part of the sentence? The time-signal word *after* tells you that the dog saw the cat first. Then he barked.

Here is another example:

Now I feel fine, but earlier I was dizzy.

Which event happened first? What happened next? The time signal words *now* and *earlier* tell you that the second part of the sentence happened first.

Use time-signal words to help you determine the order of events in this passage.

John finally came to and tried to recall what had happened. The last thing he could remember, he said, was reaching for the rope. But he had trouble recalling what had happened before that. Evidently he had slipped on the dock. Then he found himself underwater.

Which event happened first? ....

....

Which event happened next? ....

....

What happened last? ....

....

▶

The events described in the passage are not arranged in the order they happened. But the words *last, before* and *then* signaled the order of events. First John slipped on the dock. Then he found himself underwater. After that he reached for the rope. Finally he regained consciousness and tried to put the events in their proper order, much as you have done.

A Combine the two sentences below by using the time-signal words asked for.

   1. I read the book.   2. I saw the movie.

1. Use the word *then* to show that sentence 1 happened before sentence 2.

....

....

2. Use the word *before* to show that sentence 1 happened after sentence 2.

....

....

3. Use the word *after* to show that sentence 1 happened after sentence 2.

....

....

B Events in the passages that follow are not arranged in time-sequence order. Use time-signal words to help you determine the order of events. Then answer the questions after each passage.

   After a day at the beach, Paula was sunburned. She wished she had put on sun lotion when she arrived. But she had left it at home that morning.

Which event happened first? ....

....

Which event happened last? ....

....

In a moment the deer would run away. But before
that happened, Ralph took a picture. Later he would
add it to his photo album.

Which event happened first? ....

....

What would happen next? ....

....

What would happen last? ....

....

"Finally!" Kirk thought as he held his first-place
trophy high in the air. Looking at him now, it was
hard to tell he had once been overweight. First he
went on a diet. Then he started to exercise. He kept
at it, and he won the body-building contest.

What happened first? ....

....

What happened next? ....

....

What happened last? ....

....

Understanding Cause and Effect

If you see someone slip on a banana peel, you are watching an example of cause and effect. A **cause** is what makes something happen. What happens as a result of that cause is an **effect**. In this case the banana peel is the cause. Someone slipping is the effect.

What is the cause and effect in this example?

Because he stayed up late, Jack fell asleep in class.

Cause: ....

Effect: ....

Jack's staying up late was the cause of his falling asleep in class—the effect.

Sometimes an effect may be given before a cause in a sentence. For example, the sentence above might have been written this way:

Jack fell asleep in class because he stayed up late.

The cause and effect are the same as in the first example, even though the effect is written first.

Read the following sentences with cause and effect in mind.

1. Since it was my turn, I stood up to answer.
2. Because we had a rainy spring, flowers bloomed everywhere.
3. The lake freezes when the weather gets cold.
4. The store closed down as a result of the fire.

The cause came first in sentences 1 and 2. The effect came first in sentences 3 and 4.

Look for the cause and effect in each sentence below. Draw one line under the cause. Draw two lines under the effect. Check your answers against the key on page 203.

1. Jane missed the bus and was late for school.

2. Since I have a cold, I can't go to the party.

3. There was a lot of flooding from the heavy rains.

4. He hurt his finger when he tried to hammer the nail.

5. The plants died from lack of water.

Understanding Related Events

When one event causes another to happen, we say they show a **cause-and-effect relationship**. There are certain words that often signal such a relationship. The words in italics in each sentence below are cause-and-effect signal words.

1. I went to the store *because* I needed milk.
2. *Since* it is Saturday, there is no school.
3. *After* the storm, the streets were icy.
4. She was early, *so* she sat down to wait.

In each sentence, one thing caused another to happen. The signal words are clues that there is a cause-and-effect relationship.

Do not take signal words for granted, though. In some cases, there may be no cause-and-effect relationship. Look at the sentence below, for instance.

Joan ate lunch after she did her morning chores.

The two events may seem to show cause and effect, but in fact they simply follow one another. *After*, in this case, is not a time-signal word; it does not show cause and effect.

When you look for cause and effect, ask yourself these questions:

1. Does one event produce, or cause, the other?
2. Is one event the result of the other?

Only if you can answer "yes" to both of these questions is there a cause-and-effect relationship.

Put a check mark (✔) in front of each sentence that shows cause and effect.

.... 1. The sun came out when the rain stopped.
.... 2. The birds flew south and winter arrived.
.... 3. The building was destroyed because of negligence.
.... 4. Juan won a prize for selling the most tickets.

Did you check sentences 3 and 4? Both showed a cause-and-effect relationship. The two events in sentences 1 and 2 are not related in a cause-and-effect manner.

[A] Some of the sentences that follow show cause and effect. Others do not. Put a check mark (✓) in front of each sentence that does. For each sentence you checked, draw one line under the cause and two lines under the effect.

.... 1. The boys saw an animal painted on the cave wall.

.... 2. When he moved the sand, Carlos found a small box.

.... 3. Elaine, who reads quickly, finished the book.

.... 4. An eclipse occurs when the moon comes between the earth and the sun.

.... 5. The air smells fresh and clean after a rainstorm.

.... 6. Isaac Newton discovered gravity after watching an apple fall from a tree.

.... 7. It is as warm in the shade as it is in the sun.

.... 8. He got the most votes, so he is the winner.

.... 9. Jack decided to go to the library after school.

.... 10. The sound grew louder when she turned up the volume.

▶

B Complete each sentence that follows by writing an effect on the blank lines.

1. When I put an ice cube in the oven, ...

....

2. After it rained ....

....

3. ....

.... because of heavy traffic.

4. She has a cold so ....

....

C Complete each sentence that follows by writing a cause on the blank lines.

1. Sam got an "A" because ....

....

2. He smiled when ....

....

3. ....

.... they were able to see.

4. The fight started after ....

.... ■

Cause and Effect in Paragraphs

It is often easy to see cause and effect in a sentence. But finding a cause-and-effect relationship in a paragraph can be more difficult.

Read the paragraph that follows. Find the cause-and-effect relationship. Then write it on the blank lines.

> What will tomorrow's weather be like? Air masses move quickly. At the end of twenty-four hours an air mass may have moved as much as 720 miles. Because air masses move so quickly, the best way to predict the weather is by tracking their movement on a weather map.

Cause: ....

Effect: ....

The last sentence in that paragraph sums up the cause and effect. Air masses move—that is the cause. As a result, a map is used to track the movement to make predictions—that is the effect.

Sometimes the cause comes first in the paragraph, as in the example about weather. But the opposite can be true, too. Read this paragraph. Which comes first, the cause or the effect?

> Suddenly, they felt the earth tremble under their feet. The trembling was slight at first, then it grew stronger. Sarah guessed that the earth shook for about ten minutes. The next day she learned why. A major earthquake had happened!

Here the effect, trembling earth, is talked about first. The cause, an earthquake, comes at the end of the paragraph.

When looking for cause and effect, then, remember that either one may come first in a paragraph. And of course be sure that what *seems* to be a true cause-and-effect relationship really is.

▶

□ Find the cause-and-effect relationship in each paragraph below. Then write either the cause or the effect on the blank line.

Nick strolled through the park, shuffling leaves with his feet. As he passed the band shell, he was jolted out of his thoughts by the sound of screeching tires followed by a crash. He looked up to see two cars that had collided with each other. Then he looked above them, over the center of the intersection. The traffic light was out of order—both streets had green lights.

Cause: ....

Effect: Two cars had an accident.

A small spark from the campfire leaped into the night. It landed on a dry leaf and smoldered quietly. Soon a wisp of gray smoke rose in the air. Then the smoke turned to flame. It was not long before the hungry flame found other fuel. It would take hundreds of people several days to put out the forest fire.

Cause: A spark from a campfire ignited a dry leaf.

Effect: ....

One night in 1773, a group of American colonists stole on board three ships in Boston Harbor. They found the ships' cargo of tea and threw it into the water. This act was later called "The Boston Tea Party." The Americans were protesting the British tax on tea.

Cause: ....

Effect: The Boston Tea Party took place.

Joan opened her eyes. She smiled a little smile, thinking about how much she loved Saturdays. Then, just as she was about to go into a big Saturday yawn, she realized that it was Friday! She looked at her alarm clock. She was an hour late already! She jumped out of bed and jumped into her clothes. She scooped up her books and ran out the door. She kept on running all the way to school, where she burst into her classroom and blurted, "I'm sorry I'm late, Mr. Finster. My alarm didn't go off!"

Cause: Joan's alarm clock didn't go off.

Effect: .... ■

Distinguishing between Fact and Opinion

One of the sentences below is a statement of fact. The other is a statement of opinion. Can you tell the difference between them?

Florida is south of Georgia.
I think Florida is a beautiful state.

The first sentence is a statement of fact. A statement of fact is a statement about something that is supposed to be true or to have really happened. The second sentence is a statement of opinion. A statement of opinion tells what someone thinks or believes about something. Not everyone would agree that Florida is a beautiful state. People may have different opinions.

It is important to know the difference between a statement of fact and a statement of opinion. If a statement expresses an opinion, you must decide whether to agree or disagree with what it says.

For instance, if someone told you that the New York Yankees won the World Series in 1978, you might assume that to be true, or you might check the record in an almanac. But if the same person then went on to say, "The New York Yankees are the greatest baseball team ever," you might disagree. Many people might disagree, especially fans in other cities! That means the statement is an opinion.

Read each statement below. On the blank in front of the statement write *fact* if it is a statement of fact. Write *opinion* if it tells what someone thinks about something. The answers are given on page 203.

.... 1. Eating only vegetables is good for you.

.... 2. Columbus sailed to the New World in 1492.

.... 3. Charles Dickens wrote *A Tale of Two Cities*.

.... 4. Cars cost a lot of money.

.... 5. In my opinion, the speaker is right.

.... 6. Trenton is the capital of New Jersey.

Recognizing Judgment Words

Certain words and expressions are clues to opinions. Notice the words in italics in the opinions below.

1. I *think* the book is in the library.
2. That book is *exciting*.
3. It was the *best* book I ever read.
4. I *should* lend it to you.
5. You will *probably* agree.

Words such as those are **judgment words**. They make judgments about things by telling what someone thinks or feels about them. If you spot a judgment word, be prepared for an opinion.

Read statements 4 and 5 again. Statement 4 tells what someone thinks *should* happen. Statement 5 tells what someone thinks will *most likely* happen. Both are statements about the future. Since no one knows for sure what the future holds, statements about the future can only be opinions.

Opinions are frequently disguised as facts. Read this statement:

Everyone enjoyed the show.

Although it sounds like a fact, the statement is an opinion. Without taking a poll of the audience, the writer could not know that everyone enjoyed the show. Perhaps some people did not. Watch out for words such as *everyone, all, no one* and *never*. They are often used to exaggerate, or stretch, the truth. Often they hide opinions.

Statements of fact often contain clue words, too. Each word in italics in the following sentences signals a fact.

1. There are *thirty-six inches* in a yard.
2. My birthday is on *April 1*.
3. There were *twenty people* at the party.
4. They completed the building in *four months*.
5. That elephant weighs *five hundred pounds*.

Numbers such as measurements, dates and quantities frequently signal facts.

A Read the following statements to determine whether they are fact statements or opinion statements. Then write the word *fact* or *opinion* in front of each statement.

.... 1. It is the best movie I've ever seen.

.... 2. Sheldon is Todd's younger brother.

.... 3. It will probably rain tomorrow.

.... 4. Everyone likes vacations.

.... 5. Studying can be fun.

.... 6. I think we'll win the game.

.... 7. The Nile River is in Egypt.

.... 8. There are four quarts in a gallon.

.... 9. You should eat your vegetables.

.... 10. Juan's cat is named Sylvester.

B The sentences that follow are statements of opinion. Circle the clue word in each statement. Then rewrite the statement so that it gives a fact. Write the fact statement on the blank line.

1. It is a wonderful sunny day.

.... ▶

2. The bird has beautiful colored plumage.

....

3. The best way to travel is by boat.

....

4. Calvin should put his name on the list.

....

5. Rome is a fascinating city in Italy.

....

6. You are probably the first to call.

....

7. Francine is always the winner.

....

8. It was an excellent book about America's history.

....

....

Recognizing Facts and Opinions

As we have seen, there are statements of fact and there are statements of opinion. As we have also seen, sometimes it is not easy to tell the difference between the two. But it is important to develop the ability to separate facts from opinions in what we read and hear.

To be able to separate the two, we must keep in mind that a statement of fact is a statement about something that is supposed to be true or to have really happened. A statement of opinion, as we have said, tells what someone thinks, believes or feels about something.

Suppose you came across a story like the following one in a newspaper. Although it is mostly made up of facts, it does contain some opinions. Can you find them?

> In Ashland Park yesterday, the Midbury Comets defeated the Newton Sparks in the final game of the North League Softball Series. By scoring a record 27 runs, the Comets showed that they are the greatest team in league history. The Sparks managed to put just 4 runs across the plate. Their performance could only be called dismal. Comet first baseman Stan Dillon was voted Most Valuable Player of the series. For that honor, he received a free dinner at a local restaurant and a trophy donated by a local sporting-goods store.

There are two statements of opinion in the account of the game. In saying that the Comets ". . . showed that they are the greatest team in league history," the writer is expressing an opinion. The same is true for the writer's statement that the performance of the Sparks ". . . could only be called dismal." Many people who are not fans of the Comets might disagree with the statement that the Comets are the greatest team in league history. And calling the Sparks' performance "dismal" is to state an opinion. Someone else might have seen the same performance as being a "heroic effort in a losing cause." Opinions differ from person to person. They are statements of what a person thinks, feels or believes.

▶

A Read each of the following passages carefully. Then draw a line under any opinions that you find.

The weather was cool but sunny. In fact, I would say it was perfect weather for an early spring picnic. We ate fried chicken, baked beans and potato salad. Gene made lemonade. It was the best lemonade I'd ever tasted.

The rocket launch went off at 7:15 A.M. as planned. It was a glorious sight, and every last person who witnessed it was very impressed. A great cheer arose from the crowd as the rocket disappeared from sight. It was as if everyone was yelling, "See you later!" to the crew members.

The bake sale was a success. We made over fifty dollars, and that money will be used for our class party at the end of the year. But I think we'd have done even better if the sale had been last week. No one else thought that, though, so we held it yesterday.

B Now read each paragraph that follows. Decide whether it contains statements of fact or statements of opinion or both. Then circle the correct word below each paragraph.

1. Everyone knows that the earth spins on its axis. This rotation takes about twenty-four hours. It is what gives us night and day.

fact   opinion   both

2. Our school play was last Tuesday. No one was allowed in without a ticket. The actors received a standing ovation.

fact   opinion   both

3. I think you would enjoy the restaurant. It serves excellent food. The hamburgers are the best in town.

fact   opinion   both

4. It is true that February is the shortest month. But sometimes it seems to be the longest. The weather is often cold, damp and dreary.

fact   opinion   both

■

Drawing Conclusions

Suppose you are faced with the following problem. You take the bus to school every day. Today you arrive at the bus stop on time, but no one else is there. There are usually several people waiting for the bus. Your watch and the clock on the building across the street both tell the same time. You know that the bus stops here every day except on holidays.

Would you wait for the bus, or would you leave? Why? Write your answer on the blank lines.

....

....

Did you decide that the bus wasn't running because of a holiday? If so, you drew a conclusion based on the facts. You also used your knowledge about the situation to draw that conclusion.

You are often called upon to draw conclusions, which are decisions based on facts, both in your everyday life and in your reading. Most writers like to help you make connections between what has already happened and what will happen next in a story or article. They give you information and facts to help you draw conclusions as the story unfolds.

Read the following pairs of sentences. Then draw a conclusion based on the facts in those sentences. Write your conclusions on the blank lines. Check your answers against the key on page 203.

1. Swimmers can't wear cutoff jeans in the pool. Tom is swimming in the pool.

   ....

   ....

2. Tickets for the rock concert were sold out on Tuesday. Karen has two tickets for the rock concert.

   ....

   ....

3. Kites can be flown on windy days. Sam saw several people flying kites this morning.

   ....

4. Trees have leaves in summer. There are no leaves on the trees.

   ....

Drawing the Right Conclusion

Good writers like to challenge their readers. Rather than tell you everything, they give hints, or clues, about a character or an event. Like a detective, you must piece the clues together to get the whole picture.

Read the following passage. Check the conclusion that makes sense based on the clues in the passage.

> As she headed for the door, Pam grabbed her bulky backpack. As usual, she had packed too much, including an extra pair of hiking boots and an air mattress. No hard ground for her! Luckily, she did not need to pack any food. Sue, the group leader, was in charge of the week's food supplies. And Stan would be carrying the heavy pots and pans.

.... 1. Pam is weak.
.... 2. Pam is going backpacking.
.... 3. Pam is going swimming.

Did you check answer 2? The backpack, hiking boots, air mattress, and food supplies were the clues that helped you draw that conclusion. Neither of the other two conclusions makes sense.

It is important to remember that a conclusion is not a wild guess. It must be based on clues or facts. You may also need to use your knowledge or experience to draw a conclusion. Since the passage did not mention that Pam was going camping, you had to use your knowledge of that activity to draw the best conclusion.

When you draw conclusions, be careful to examine the facts carefully. If you don't think carefully, you may reach a false conclusion. For example, look at the facts below.

> Some airplane pilots are under thirty.
> Some airplane pilots are over fifty.

From those facts, someone might come to the conclusion that all airplane pilots are either under thirty or over fifty. That would be a false conclusion. There are, of course, many pilots between the ages of thirty and fifty. Too few facts are given to reach a conclusion.

Watch out for conclusions that use words like *all, every, only* and *always*. Those words often signal false conclusions.

☐ Read the following passages carefully. Then, before each statement, write *true* if the statement is a true conclusion. Write *false* if it is not.

Once, Hollywood was the center of filmmaking in the United States. Moviemakers seldom went outside the city. Elaborate sets were built right at the studios. Today, though, moviemakers use other places. As one person explained, "Other cities are a lot cheaper and a lot less trouble."

.... 1. Hollywood is no longer the center of filmmaking in the United States.

.... 2. No films are made in Hollywood these days.

.... 3. People in Hollywood are greedy.

.... 4. The cost of making movies in Hollywood is too high for some moviemakers.

.... 5. It is often easier to make movies outside of Hollywood.

Evening came to the countryside. Brian hurried to finish his letters as the light grew dimmer. One letter was to Joan, the other to his mother. His mother was growing old, and she would miss him. But Joan would understand why he had to leave. Ever since their father died, nothing had seemed to go right. Brian leaned his head against the window and sighed. He tried to sleep, but the rhythmic *clickety-clack* of the wheels kept him awake.

▶

.... 1. Brian is on an airplane.

.... 2. Joan is Brian's sister.

.... 3. The events take place late at night.

.... 4. Brian has no brothers.

.... 5. Brian is on a train.   ■

Looking for Important Facts

Sometimes you need all the facts in a passage in order to draw a conclusion. But often a passage contains more information than you need. Then you have to decide which facts are necessary to reach a conclusion.

Read the following passage and put a check mark (✓) beside the best conclusion.

Carl was a real showman. Before every throw, he went into his act. Holding the ball in his fingertips, he would switch it back and forth in front of his face, as if he wanted to check it out. That done, he would cover the ball with his glove and hold it against his chest while he looked at each base in turn. Finally, he shuffled his feet. That was a signal to the catcher that the pitch was on its way. Of course, the routine drove the batters crazy. Carl loved every minute of it.

.... 1. Carl is an actor.

.... 2. Carl is a baseball pitcher.

.... 3. Carl is a first-baseman.

.... 4. Carl is a football player.

If you checked answer 2, you drew the right conclusion. But you did not need all the information in the passage to reach that conclusion. For instance, you did not need to know that Carl was a showman or that he shuffled his feet. Those facts add interest to the passage, but they do not help you conclude that Carl is a pitcher.

Reread the paragraph to find the important facts. Circle only those facts that are necessary to reach the conclusion that Carl is a baseball pitcher.

▶

A Look for the important facts as you read the passages that follow. Then below each one, put a check mark (✓) in front of each conclusion that you can draw from the passage.

Shivering, I left the chilled cabin in search of Jim. It was as if he had read my mind. There he was in the barnyard, chopping wood. Although Jim had worked for my family for as long as I could remember, I was always amazed at his size. He was well over six feet tall. He had huge, broad shoulders. His arms were three times the size of mine, and his legs reminded me of tree trunks. Years of hard labor had weathered his hands, and his face was as brown and wrinkled as an old shoe. He nodded toward the cabin. "I figured you'd be needing some wood," he said.

.... 1. Jim is a weight lifter.
.... 2. Jim is chopping wood for a fire.
.... 3. Jim is chopping wood to build a house.
.... 4. Jim is a laborer.
.... 5. The scene takes place in the country.

The world's first great fossil hunter was a French-man named Georges Cuvier. In the beginning, Cuvier wanted to study living animals. Then, in 1795, he discovered some ancient bones buried in the soil in Paris. Much to his surprise, they proved to be ele-phant bones! But they were not like the bones of modern elephants. These bones had belonged to a somewhat different creature—an ancestor of the modern elephant. To the people of Paris, Cuvier's find was incredible.

.... 1. A fossil is the remains of an animal from long ago.
.... 2. There are no elephants in Paris today.
.... 3. Ancestors of today's elephants once roamed the area around Paris.
.... 4. Fossils are living animals.
.... 5. Cuvier is the only person to have found fossils.

B Read the following passage. Then put an **X** in the box beside the best conclusion.

A warm, sticky day can make the folks in Kansas a little nervous. They know that it could mark the start of a tornado. The warm, moist air at ground level will rise quickly. Cooler air will then rush in to take its place. When it heats up, it too will rise. All that moving air can turn into a funnel-shaped cloud. If the cloud dips low enough, it will stir up dirt and debris. The force of the swirling wind can become great enough to blow down everything in its path. That is a tornado. A tornado starts out with a hissing sound that grows into a loud roar. Many people have compared the sound to that of a charging railroad train. Tornadoes are deadly and destructive. The only good thing that can be said about them is that they are usually brief.

The passage leads us to conclude that tornadoes
- ☐ a. form only in hot weather.
- ☐ b. can be prevented.
- ☐ c. are not so bad once you get to know them.
- ☐ d. arrive in the afternoon.

Now write in your own words three ideas from the passage that led you to your conclusion.

1. ....

....

2. ....

....

3. ....

....

Comprehension Skills Achievement Test

I. Main Idea

A. Underline the sentence that states the main idea in each group of sentences below.

1. People have played pranks on that day for hundreds of years.
   No one knows how the idea of April Fool's Day began.
   On that day people play jokes on other people.
   The first day of April is called April Fool's Day.

2. The Wright brothers flew a plane called the "Flyer."
   On December 17, 1903, people flew for the first time.
   Orville Wright flew for 12 seconds.
   Wilbur Wright flew for 59 seconds.

3. Apes belong to the same group of mammals that humans belong to.
   Apes are very intelligent.
   Of all our animal relatives, apes are most like humans.
   Some apes walk erect, much as we do.

4. Alchemists were not good scientists.
   Magic played a large part in alchemy.
   The chemistry of the Middle Ages was called alchemy.
   Alchemists dreamed they could change common metals into gold.

B. The paragraphs below lack unity. Underline the sentence in each paragraph that does not support the main idea. Then below each paragraph, put a check mark (✓) beside the main idea.

1. Shelter was one of the first needs the pioneers had to meet. Once a good spot for a cabin was selected, the work of building began. The great hope of the pioneers was to obtain a better life through owning their own farms. Settlers could usually depend on neighbors to lend a hand.

.... a. Pioneer problems
.... b. Pioneer shelters
.... c. Owning a farm

2. Getting a breath of fresh air used to mean simply breathing outdoors. But today, thanks to pollution, the air outdoors is far from fresh in many cases. Enormous amounts of wastes are being sent into it. The name for one form of pollution, smog, is created by combining two words—*smoke* and *fog*.

.... a. Smog
.... b. Waste
.... c. Air pollution

II. Sequence

Underline the time-signal words in each group of sentences. Then follow the directions below each group of sentences.

1. After the game ended, the crowd left quickly. Then the players had a party.

   Write *1* by the event that happened first. Write *2* by the event that happened next.

.... a. The game ended.
.... b. The crowd left.
.... c. The players had a party.

2. Carol was looking the other way when the ball hit her. Later she had to go to the hospital.

   Write *1* next to the events that happened at the same time. Write *2* next to the event that happened last.

.... a. Carol was looking the other way.
.... b. The ball hit her.
.... c. She went to the hospital.

3. Sam went to the library before it got dark. It was eight o'clock when he left the library.

Write *1* next to the event that happened first. Write *2* next to the event that happened next. Write *3* next to the two events that happened last.

.... a. Sam went to the library.
.... b. It got dark.
.... c. Sam left the library.
.... d. It was eight o'clock.

4. Manuel and I went to the movies last night. But first we had to do our chores. I washed the floor while Manuel did the dishes.

Write *1* by the events that happened at the same time. Write *2* by the event that happened last.

.... a. We went to the movies.
.... b. I washed the floor.
.... c. Manuel did the dishes.

5. Now the men looked worn and hopeless. But once they had been young and carefree. The loss of their farms followed by the death of their loved ones had left them bitter.

Number the events from *1* to *4* in time-sequence order.

.... a. The men looked worn and hopeless.
.... b. The men were young and carefree.
.... c. The men lost their farms.
.... d. Their loved ones died.

III. Cause and Effect

A. Some of the sentences below show cause and effect while others do not. Put a check mark (✔) in front of each sentence that does. For each sentence you check, draw one line under the cause and two lines under the effect.

.... 1. The Alps, which are the highest mountains in Europe, are ten million years old.
.... 2. After Jake got cold, he went inside.
.... 3. He admitted his guilt, then watched TV.

.... 4. If you want to enjoy yourself, take a vacation.

.... 5. Lemons are sour because they have acid in them.

.... 6. Since it is not often played with other instruments, an accordian is called a solo instrument.

.... 7. After the sun came out, the air felt warmer.

.... 8. Alligators and crocodiles are often mistaken for each other because they look so much alike.

.... 9. The word *electricity* comes from the Greek word for "amber."

.... 10. A bottle of air looks empty because air is invisible.

B. Find the cause-and-effect relationship in each paragraph that follows. Then check the statement that best expresses that relationship.

1.   Many people who like the taste of certain foods never eat them. They know that they are likely to become sick if they do. These people have what are called allergies. Different people are allergic to different foods.

.... a. Some people are allergic to certain foods.
.... b. People often get sick.
.... c. Allergies are the result of stress.

2. Imagine a very heavy weight hung from a strong wire. You would have to push hard to start it swinging. Once it was swinging, it would need a large force to stop it. That is because of inertia, which makes all matter resist a change in its motion. The heavier the object, the greater the force you will need to start or stop its movement.

.... a. Heavy weights are hard to move.
.... b. Force is the result of inertia.
.... c. Inertia causes matter to resist a change in its motion.

IV. Fact and Opinion

A. Write *F* in front of each statement that is a fact. Write *O* in front of each statement that is an opinion. Circle the clue words that signal opinions.

.... 1. No one likes a poor loser.

.... 2. Trees are the oldest plants.

.... 3. The letter *a* has several different sounds.

.... 4. That book probably belongs to Mark.

.... 5. Everyone should be careful about using medicines.

.... 6. Some people have weird superstitions.

.... 7. Mountain climbing is fun.

.... 8. Some seaweeds can be eaten.

.... 9. I think the scenery is beautiful.

.... 10. Alexander the Great lived more than two thousand years ago.

B. Read each paragraph that follows. Decide whether it contains statements of fact or statements of opinion or both. Then circle the correct word below each paragraph.

1. I think you would like the play. All the actors deliver great performances. The playwright, too, is a young talent to watch.

      fact   opinion   both

2. The sun rose at 6:58 this morning. It was the most beautiful sunrise of the year. The forecast states that the sun will rise at 7:00 A.M. tomorrow.

      fact   opinion   both

3. The moon's gravity is weaker than that of earth. It would be fun to jump around on the moon, because you could jump very high.

      fact   opinion   both

4. The weather around the equator is usually hot. People who live on or near the equator gear their lifestyles around that hot weather.

fact   opinion   both

V. Conclusions

Read the passages below. Put a check mark (✔) by each conclusion you can draw from the passage.

A. Good students take advantage of the aids offered in textbooks. Headings are one important aid. They help you see how material is organized and how one section relates to the next. Another valuable aid is the use of boldfaced type to highlight certain terms and ideas.

.... a. Students who do not use textbook aids do not do well in school.
.... b. Textbook aids can be helpful.
.... c. Good students are far and few between.
.... d. All textbooks provide aids.
.... e. Headings are necessary to organize material.

B. Heavy snow and freezing rain had fallen the day before. Driving was hazardous. Nevertheless, Scott drove along at sixty miles an hour. He had a daredevil streak in his nature. In fact, the idea of becoming a stock-car racer had crossed his mind more than once. Suddenly, his right front tire hit an icy patch and his car began to skid.

.... a. Scott was driving too fast for the conditions.
.... b. Scott was a poor driver.
.... c. Some stock-car racers are daredevils.
.... d. Scott is driving during the winter.
.... e. Scott will become a stock-car racer.

Developing Reference Skills

Using a Library

Did you ever wish you could know everything in the world? Of course, that would be impossible. But you can have the world's knowledge at your fingertips. How? By visiting a library. A library is a great resource. It contains information on almost every subject you can think of. Much of this information is in books. But there is also much information to be found in magazines, newspapers, filmstrips, pictures, tapes and records. All of those are yours to use—for free! But in order to take advantage of all that knowledge, you must know how to find what you want.

A good library will be organized in a way that makes things easy to find. No two libraries are exactly alike, but most share a similar arrangement. Often a library will have a map posted near the door. That helps you find your way even in a library you've never visited before. The map below is one example of how a library can be organized.

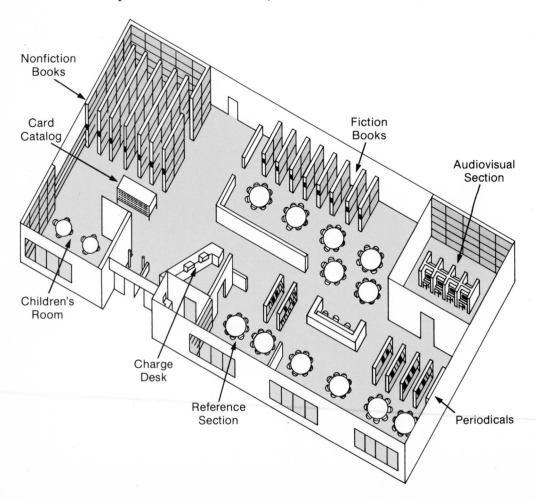

If you want a fiction or nonfiction book, your first stop should be the **card catalog**. It tells what books the library has. From there you can look for the book on the shelves. If you want to use a dictionary or other reference book, you can go straight to the **reference** section. Magazines and newspapers are in the **periodicals** section. You can expect to find records and tapes in the **audiovisual** section. If you have trouble finding what you want, the librarian is always there to help.

Now answer the following questions about what you have just read. Write your answers on the blank lines. Then check them against the answer key on page 204.

1. Where would you check to see whether a library has a certain book? ....

2. Why do you think most libraries are organized in much the same way? ....

....

3. In what section of the library would you expect to find filmstrips? ....

4. If you have trouble finding what you want, what should you do? ....

Making Use of Reference Books

When you hear the term reference book, what do you think of? If you are like many people, you think of a dictionary or an encyclopedia. But there are other types of reference books. In fact, we can divide all reference books into two groups.

First, there is the large group of reference books that each contain information on a specific subject. This group includes such books as dictionaries, encyclopedias, atlases and almanacs.

The books in the second group tell you where to find information in the first group. This second group is made up of indexes, bibliographies and other such books. If you need information on a certain subject, you first look up that subject in one of these references. There you will learn where the information you need is located in the books in the first group.

You cannot check reference books out of the library. They are meant to be used as tools. You should consult them to find the information you need. Then return them to the shelf.

Each reference book has its own organization. Before you use one, look at its table of contents. That will tell you how the book, or set of books, is arranged. In the front of most reference books you will find an explanation of how to use them.

Each reference book serves a certain purpose. Below is a list of the most common types of reference books. Learn what makes each one different from the other.

dictionaries—information about words
encyclopedias—general articles on many subjects
atlases—maps and charts
almanacs—general facts and lists
indexes—location of needed information
bibliographies—lists of books
directories—names and addresses of people and groups
gazetteers—dictionaries of geographical information
yearbooks—the year's events in brief form

A Column A lists ten reference books. Column B lists what is covered by those reference books. On the blank line before each book in column A, write the letter of its function in column B.

A   **B**

.... dictionary   a. location of needed information

.... encyclopedia   b. past year's events in brief

.... atlas   c. lists of books

.... almanac   d. general facts, lists

.... index   e. names and addresses

.... yearbook   f. information about words

.... bibliography   g. maps and charts

.... directory   h. general articles on many subjects

.... gazetteer   i. geographical information

B Circle the reference book in each pair that you would use *first* to find information on each of the following topics.

1. how to spell a word   dictionary
                                        encyclopedia

2. the states that border New Mexico   atlas
                                        yearbook

3. where to locate needed information   handbook
                                        index   ▶

4. the longest river in the world

atlas
almanac

5. background on space travel

directory
encyclopedia

6. the location of Ellis Island

gazetteer
bibliography

7. a list of the world's tallest buildings

almanac
dictionary

8. the address of the A.S.P.C.A.

atlas
directory

9. the definition of *reference*

dictionary
encyclopedia

10. a list of mystery books

bibliography
directory

11. geographical information on Alaska

gazetteer
index

12. a list of the past year's events

encyclopedia
yearbook

13. a map showing world transportation

gazetteer
atlas

14. a list of holidays

almanac
gazetteer

■

Making Use of Periodicals

Suppose you want to know about an event that took place a few months ago. Or you want to read about a certain subject that is of special interest to you. What you need is a specific, up-to-date source: a **periodical**. Where do you find periodicals?

The Periodicals Room. Most libraries have a room devoted strictly to periodicals, which are magazines and newspapers that are published on a daily, weekly, monthly or twice-monthly basis. All the magazines and newspapers that a library makes available are kept in the periodicals room. The current issues are on shelves or racks, displayed where they are easy to find. Back issues are usually put in boxes and stored. The librarian is in charge of locating back issues.

Reference Tools for Periodicals. Naturally, it would take a long time to search through all the periodicals a library keeps. So, there are special indexes to help you find what you want. One is the *Readers' Guide to Periodical Literature*. It is a listing of more than one hundred and fifty magazines and the articles that are in them. It is published several times a year, so it is quite up-to-date.

Each entry in the *Readers' Guide* lists the title of the article, the author's name, the volume number of the magazine the article is in, and the magazine's page numbers on which the article can be found. It also lists the magazine's publication date, and tells you if the article has illustrations.

Some large newspapers have their own index. The *New York Times Index* is one example. It tells the date of the issue of the *Times* in which an article appeared, and the page and the column where the article can be found.

Since storage space is a problem, many libraries keep only the more recent issues in the periodicals section. Older issues may be stored elsewhere. If you want an issue that is not on the shelves, ask the librarian to find it for you.

Some libraries keep periodicals on **microfilm**. That is a tiny picture of printed pages on film. It requires a special viewer that enlarges, or magnifies, the words. Your librarian can explain how to use the microfilm system.

▶

A Write answers to the following questions on the blank lines.

1. What is a periodical? ....

....

....

2. Where in a library are current magazines and newspapers

kept? ....

3. List three of your favorite magazines. ....

....

....

4. Write the names of two newspapers. ....

....

5. Where should you look to find an article in a magazine?

....

....

6. Why do libraries use microfilm? ....

7. How many magazines are indexed in the *Readers' Guide to*

Periodical Literature? ....

8. Name one way in which the *Readers' Guide* and a card

catalog are alike. ....

....

B Look at the following section from the *Readers' Guide to Periodical Literature.* Then answer the questions that follow.

Subject entry ——————┐   ┌—————————— Authors

    HAWAII
        We've lost the aloha feeling. J. Kelly and M. Moritz. il
        Time 117:29 Je 1 '81

    HAWAIIAN Islands. See Hawaii

Author entry ——— **HAWKINS, William J.**
        Look and listen [cont] il Pop Sci 218:25 My '81

Article title ——————————————————┘
Illustrated ——————————————————————— Date of issue
Magazine ——————————————————————— Magazine page number
                                                                    Magazine volume number

1. What are the two subject entries?

   ....

2. What other kind of entry can you find in the *Reader's Guide?*

   ....

3. On what page of *Time* does the article on Hawaii appear?

   ....

4. What is the name of the article by William J. Hawkins?

   ....

5. In what month's issue of *Popular Science* does that article appear?

   ....

Using a Dictionary

A dictionary is much more than just an alphabetical listing of words. If you know how to use it well, it can answer many questions. It tells how a word is spelled, pronounced and defined. It may use the word in a sentence. Sometimes it gives a word's **origin**, or where and when it was first used. It may give **synonyms**, or words that have the same meaning, and **antonyms**, which are words that have opposite meanings. Illustrations such as pictures, charts and maps may be included too. When you use a dictionary, you learn about more than just words. You also learn a bit about people, places and events.

Some dictionaries are **unabridged**. That is, they list almost all the words in a language. Others are **abridged**; they are shorter versions with fewer words. There are also those that deal with only one part of a language—word history, for instance, or words and terms used in business.

No two dictionaries are alike. Each has its own special features. To find a dictionary that you like, ask yourself these questions about each dictionary you inspect:

1. What type of dictionary is it?
2. Are the definitions clear?
3. Does it show the division of syllables?
4. Is the pronunciation guide clear and easy to use?
5. Does it explain the origin or history of a word?
6. Are there sentences to show how to use a word?
7. Does it give synonyms and antonyms?
8. Does it contain illustrations?
9. Is it easy to use?

Answering those questions can help you choose the dictionary that is best for you.

Read each following statement, then write *true* if the statement is true and *false* if the statement is false. Check your answers against the key on page 204.

.... 1. A dictionary lists words in alphabetical order.

.... 2. An abridged dictionary has fewer words than an unabridged dictionary.

.... 3. All dictionaries give synonyms and antonyms.

.... 4. Some dictionaries include maps.

.... 5. A dictionary defines words.

.... 6. Synonyms are words that have the same meaning.

.... 7. Dictionaries show how to pronounce words.

.... 8. The definition of a word is the same as its origin.

Reading a Dictionary Entry

The words defined in a dictionary are called **entry words**. They are printed in heavy black type called **boldface**.

Look at this entry from the *Scott, Foresman Intermediate Dictionary:*

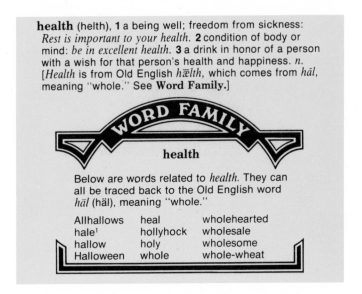

health (helth), **1** a being well; freedom from sickness: *Rest is important to your health.* **2** condition of body or mind: *be in excellent health.* **3** a drink in honor of a person with a wish for that person's health and happiness. *n.* [*Health* is from Old English *hǣlth*, which comes from *hāl*, meaning "whole." See **Word Family**.]

WORD FAMILY

health

Below are words related to *health*. They can all be traced back to the Old English word *hāl* (häl), meaning "whole."

Allhallows	heal	wholehearted
hale¹	hollyhock	wholesale
hallow	holy	wholesome
Halloween	whole	whole-wheat

After the entry word *health* is its pronunciation in parentheses. A definition of the word follows. And since *health* has more than one meaning, two more numbered definitions are included. In the *Scott, Foresman* dictionary the most common meaning is given first. To help make each meaning clear, the word is used in a phrase or a sentence.

After the definitions is the abbreviation *n.* This tells you that the word *health* is a noun. The other parts of speech are abbreviated as shown:

adjective	*adj.*
adverb	*adv.*
verb	*v.*
pronoun	*pron.*
conjunction	*conj.*
interjection	*interj.*
preposition	*prep.*

The history of the word *health* is given in brackets. It tells you when and where the word was first used, how it was originally spelled, and what it meant.

This dictionary has one special feature, too. It points out other words that belong to the same word group, or family. How many words are listed?

[A] Below are six entries from a dictionary. Read the entries and then answer the questions that follow.

midge (mij), a small two-winged fly; gnat. *n.*

head stone (hed′stōn′), stone set at the head of a grave; gravestone. *n.*

Hu go (hyü′gō), **Victor,** 1802-1885, French writer of poetry, novels, and plays. *n.*

bug gy (bug′ē), **1** a light carriage with or without a top, pulled by one horse and having a single large seat. **2** a baby's carriage. *n., pl.* **bug gies.**

Mi ner va (mə nėr′və), (in Roman myths) the goddess of wisdom, the arts, and war. The Greeks called her Athena. *n.*

cen., central.

From *Scott, Foresman Intermediate Dictionary*

1. Which entry word names an object found in a cemetery?

   ....

2. Which is the name of a writer? ....

3. Which can you ride in? ....

4. Which one flies? ....

5. Which one has another name? ....

6. Which one is an abbreviation? .... ▶

[B] Read the entry from the *Scott, Foresman Intermediate Dictionary* for the word *caution*. Then answer the questions that follow.

cau tion (kô′shən), **1** great care; regard for safety; unwillingness to take chances: *Always use caution when crossing streets.* **2** a warning: *A sign with "Danger" on it is a caution.* **3** urge to be careful; warn: *I cautioned them against playing in the street.* 1,2 *n.,* 3 *v.*

From *Scott, Foresman Intermediate Dictionary*

1. How is *caution* pronounced? ....

2. How many definitions are given? ....

3. Which definition is the most common? ....

4. What is the part of speech abbreviation for the entry word when it is used as a noun in definition 2? ....

5. What is the definition of *caution* when it is used as a verb (*v*)?

....   ■

Using Pronunciations

It would be easy to pronounce words if each letter of the alphabet had only one sound. But there are more than forty sounds in the English language, and only twenty-six letters in the alphabet.

What is more, a sound is not always spelled the same way. Read the words below, for instance.

ate	break	grey	train
weight	stay	rein	

All of the words contain the same sound—the pronunciation of the name of the letter *A*. This is called *long a*. But the sound is spelled differently in each word.

Dictionaries use symbols to help you pronounce words. There is one symbol for each sound. Here is how the dictionary would give the pronunciations for the words above.

ate (**āt**)   weight (**wāt**)
break (**brāk**)   stay (**stā**)
grey (**grā**)   rein (**rān**)
train (**trān**)

Notice that in each one, the long *a* sound is shown as **ā**. To find out which symbols stand for which sounds, you need to look at a **pronunciation key**. Here is one key.

a hat	i it	oi oil	ch child	a in about
ā age	ī ice	ou out	ng long	e in taken
ä far	o hot	u cup	sh she	ə = { i in pencil
e let	ō open	ù put	th thin	o in lemon
ē equal	ô order	ü rule	ŦH then	u in circus
ėr term			zh measure	

From Scott, Foresman Intermediate Dictionary

Look at the first symbol **a** and *hat*, the word that follows it. *Hat* is called a **key word**. It tells you that whenever you see the symbol **a** in a pronunciation, you say the same sound that you say for the letter *a* in *hat*.

Notice the symbol **e** and its five key words. When you say the key words, you make the same sound for the *a* in *about*, the *e* in *taken*, the *i* in *pencil*, the *o* in *lemon*, and the *u* in *circus*.

▶

Another way the dictionary helps you pronounce words is by dividing them into syllables. For instance, the entry word *shadow* looks like this:

shad ow (shad′o)

Shadow has two syllables. Notice the accent mark after the first syllable in the pronunciation. This tells you to say that syllable **shad** more forcefully than the other. If a word has more than two syllables, more accent marks may be used. For example:

dic tion ar y (dik′ shə ner′ ē)

The word *dictionary* has four syllables. The dark accent after the first syllable tells you to stress it. The light accent after the third syllable tells you to say it more strongly than the two unaccented syllables, but not as strongly as the first.

a hat	**i** it	**oi** oil	**ch** child	a in about
ā age	**ī** ice	**ou** out	**ng** long	e in taken
ä far	**o** hot	**u** cup	**sh** she	ə = { i in pencil
e let	**ō** open	**u̇** put	**th** thin	o in lemon
ē equal	**ô** order	**ü** rule	**ŦH** then	u in circus
ėr term			**zh** measure	

From *Scott, Foresman Intermediate Dictionary*

A One word in each group has a different sound for the same letters. Pronounce each word aloud. Then circle the word in each group that does not belong.

1. Which word does not have the sound ā?

agent   am   bake   stay

2. Which word does have the sound ī?

bin   within   fight   chimney

3. Which word does not have the sound ô?

border   office   on   tone

4. Which word does not have the sound ŦH?

brother   think   smooth   rather

5. Which word does not have the sound **sh**?

shirt   school   shop   worship

B Each of the numbered pronunciations stands for a word. Write the word from the list below next to its pronunciation. Use the pronunciation key to help you.

cease	hope	back	buck
says	cause	chore	so
hoop	hurt	heart	crease

1. bak _____

2. hüp _____

3. sēs _____

4. chôr _____

5. kôz _____

6. hōp _____

7. krēs _____

8. buk _____

9. sez _____

10. härt _____

11. sō _____

12. hėrt _____

C The words below are divided into syllables. Say each word to yourself. Then put the accent mark after the syllable you say the strongest.

1. crack er

2. li on

3. ex cit ing

4. out fit

5. de ny

6. brav er y

7. ex am

8. fa mous ly

9. fan tas tic

Using an Encyclopedia

The word *encyclopedia* comes from two ancient Greek words. The words are *enkyklios*, which means "general," and *paideia*, which means "education." This reference is one of the library's most useful books. Of course, no book can contain all there is to know about a subject. But an encyclopedia is a good place to start when you are looking for information.

Most of the time you will use a general encyclopedia. This is usually a set of books, or volumes, that gives overviews of a wide range of subjects. Some you might find in the library are the *World Book Encyclopedia, Compton's Encyclopedia,* the *Encyclopedia Americana* and the *Encyclopaedia Britannica.* Each one has special features. *Compton's,* for instance, is noted for its pictures, maps and charts. The *World Book* is easy to read. Both are good for young readers.

There are also **special subject encyclopedias**. Such an encyclopedia deals with only one subject, such as art or science, for example, and is often only one volume.

If you are using an encyclopedia for the first time, read the introduction carefully. It will explain:

> **Organization**. How many subjects does it cover? How much detail does it include in its articles?
>
> **Arrangement**. Is there one volume or are there many? Are the subjects general or detailed?
>
> **Index**. Is the index very detailed? Is there a single index or one for each book?
>
> **Special Features**. Is there a list of related topics at the end of some articles? Are some articles outlined? Is there a list of books at the end of the article you can refer to for more information?

When you know the answers to these questions, you will be able to make better use of an encyclopedia.

Now answer the questions that follow. Write your answers on the blank lines. Then check them against the answer key on page 204.

1. What does the word *encyclopedia* mean?

   ....

2. What is a general encyclopedia? ....

   ....

   ....

3. Name two general encyclopedias.

   ....

4. Why do you think there are encyclopedias on only one subject?

   ....

   ....

5. Why should you read the introduction to an encyclopedia?

   ....

   ....

Tips for Using an Encyclopedia

You have probably used an encyclopedia before. But have you always made the most of it? The following tips may help you make better use of this important reference:

- Use it as a starting place. Remember that an encyclopedia does not tell everything about a subject. The articles may be brief. They may answer the questions *Who? What? When? Where?* and *How?* but leave *Why?* unanswered.

- Look at the arrangement. Is there one or are there many volumes? Knowing the arrangement will help you find your subject more quickly. Suppose you want to know about roses, for example. In some encyclopedias, you would find it under the subject heading ROSE. In others, it might be under the broader subject heading FLOWER.

- Choose the right word. When you look for a subject, make sure you look for it under the right word. For instance, if you want to know about the history of skiing, look in the *S* volume under SKIING, not in the *H* volume under HISTORY. If the subject is a person, look under the last name. For information on Robert E. Lee, for example, you would look under LEE.

- Use the guide words. After you have chosen the correct volume, use the guide words at the top of each page. They can save you a lot of time.

- Use the index. An encyclopedia of only one volume will have an index at the back. In an encyclopedia that consists of several volumes, one volume will serve as the index for the entire set.

A Choose the word you would look under for each topic in an encyclopedia and write it on the line.

.... 1. rules for bicycle safety

.... 2. volcano eruptions

.... 3. automobile manufacturing

.... 4. President George Washington

.... 5. mountain ranges

.... 6. the history of television

.... 7. the Grand Canyon

.... 8. Nobel Prize winners

.... 9. junior high schools

.... 10. Albert Einstein

.... 11. the causes of the Civil War

.... 12. the state of Alaska

.... 13. the first museum in America

.... 14. cures for diseases ▶

B On the blank line, write the answer to each question.

1. Why is an encyclopedia a starting place for information?

....

....

2. What five questions does an encyclopedia answer?

....

....

3. What question is often not answered by an encyclopedia?

....

4. What can be found at the top of each encyclopedia page to help you find your topic?

....

5. For an encyclopedia with several volumes, where are you likely to find the index?

....

....

How to Read an Encyclopedia Article

Do you know how to get the most from an encyclopedia article?

First take a quick look at the article. Does it cover the subject at length, or is it a short article?

Next glance at the headings. They will give you a good idea of the facts that are covered. Look at these headings from an article on Africa:

THE LAND
THE PEOPLE
THE NATURAL WEALTH
MANUFACTURING AND MINING
TRANSPORTATION

Headings like these will tell you whether the article has the kind of information you need. You could expect this article to talk about Africa's crops, for example, under NATURAL WEALTH.

When you decide that an article is useful, read it carefully. Take brief notes about the main facts and ideas. Sometimes an outline at the beginning or end of a long article will point out the main topics covered. There may also be a list of questions about the article. Use them to test yourself on how well you understood the content.

Study any illustrations. Pictures, charts and maps can be quite useful. They help to explain the text.

There is often a list of related topics at the end of an article. You can look up those other topics for facts on your subject. For instance, you might find the following topics listed after an article on literature:

BOOK   NOBEL PRIZES
LIBRARY   READING
LANGUAGE   WRITING

You would look for those under the first letter of each topic.

Sometimes you may find a list of books at the end of an article. This list is called a **bibliography**. The books will be useful if you need more information than the article gives. Look for them in the card catalog of your library.

▶

☐ Look at the page on the right from the *World Book Encyclopedia*. Fill in the answers on the blank lines.

1. The article is about ....

....

2. The article discusses two ways in which animals live together. What are they?

....

....

3. According to the article, animals that live together usually

eat ....

4. What does the picture on the right-hand side of the page show?

....

....

5. The picture at the bottom of the page shows some prairie dogs and describes

....

....

6. How do you think the prairie dogs keep their grass cut short?

....

....

Animals That Live Together

Animals that need not fear each other often live together in groups. Such animals usually eat plants and do not hunt other animals for food.

Flocks and Herds. Birds and mammals sometimes live together in flocks or herds of their own kind. These groups are often called *communities*. In most flocks or groups of animals, a few members become leaders and the others remain followers. The followers may do work that helps the group. Some keep watch for enemies while the rest of the group eats or sleeps.

In most groups, a leader holds its place by fighting. The leading bull of a buffalo herd must be able to defeat all the other bulls in the herd. Chickens and some other birds have a "pecking order." Every member of the flock fights for its place in the pecking order. Each chicken eats or drinks ahead of all the other chickens that it can peck. But it steps aside for any chicken that can peck it.

Some insects live in colonies. They organize their colonies in special ways. Ants and bees have queens that lay all the eggs, and workers that gather food for the colony. Among some ants, certain workers with powerful jaws fight the colony's battles.

Some animals live so closely together that they form what seems to be a single animal. The Portuguese man-of-war, a jellyfish, is really a group of as many as a hundred different animals. Each of the animals has a certain job to do. Some find food, some fight enemies, and some produce young.

Animal Partnerships. Sometimes different kinds of animals help each other and even become partners. Small birds called crocodile birds help crocodiles get rid of certain enemies. The birds feed on insects that live on the crocodiles' bodies. Some zoologists say that the birds even hop into the mouth of a crocodile and eat the bloodsucking leeches that cling between the crocodile's teeth. In this partnership, the birds find food, and the crocodile gets rid of pests. Other small birds ride on the backs of antelope and elephants, eating ticks and insects that bite the large animals. The birds also warn their partners of danger. When they see an enemy coming toward one side of the large animal, they all move to its other side. Or they fly away. The movements of the birds warn the antelope or elephant to flee.

Walter Dawn, NAS

Animal Partnerships benefit both animals. For example, birds called egrets feed on insects stirred up by grazing cattle. In return, the egret warns the cattle of danger by flying away.

J. W. Jackson

The Neighbors. Prairie dogs live in "towns" made up of burrows a few yards apart. The animals keep the grass around the burrows cut short so that an enemy can easily be seen. Some members of the community act as sentries and give warning when danger is near. Then all the prairie dogs run into their burrows to wait until the enemy goes away.

Using an Almanac

An almanac is a quick reference source. That is, you can use it to find certain kinds of facts quickly.

The word *almanac* comes from an Arabic word meaning "calendar." And that is what the first almanacs were. They served as calendars of the months. They gave information on eclipses, planet movements, and the rising and setting times of the sun, moon and stars.

Today's almanacs are much more. They are handy references for a wide range of facts. You can find the answers to thousands of questions in an almanac. And, because almanacs are published once a year, they keep facts up-to-date.

Two of the most widely used almanacs are *The World Almanac and Book of Facts* and the *Information Please Almanac.* Both contain short, easy-to-read articles, but most of the information is in the form of lists and charts that give facts at a glance.

The topics in an almanac are not in alphabetical order, as they are in most other reference books. So you must use the index to find the facts you want. *The World Almanac*, for instance, has a General Index in the front of the book and a Quick Reference Index in the back. The General Index gives a detailed list of topics and subtopics, with page numbers for each entry. The Quick Reference Index, on the other hand, directs you to very general topic areas. A Quick Reference entry might read like this: Nutrition, pp. 132–135. Once you turn to that section you have to leaf through the pages listed to find the specific bit of information you want.

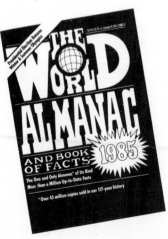
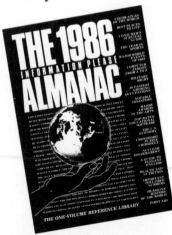

You can use an almanac to answer questions like these:

1. Who won the World Series last year?
2. What are the world's ten tallest buildings?
3. What is the population of Tokyo, Japan?
4. Who are the senators from your state?
5. How do people spend their money?
6. What is the distance between Miami, Florida, and Houston, Texas?

Now answer these questions about what you have just read. Write your answers on the blank lines. Then check them against the answer key on page 204.

1. Why is an almanac a quick reference source?

....

....

2. How often are almanacs published? ....

3. How can you find information in an almanac?

....

4. Write two questions an almanac can answer.

....

....

....

Reading Lists and Charts

Much of the information in an almanac is in the form of lists and charts. You can get facts quickly from such sources.

The list below, from the *Information Please Almanac*, is much like other lists you will find in an almanac.

Firsts in America

Admiral in U.S. Navy: David Glasgow Farragut, 1866.

Air-mail route, first transcontinental: Between New York City and San Francisco, 1920.

Assembly, representative: House of Burgesses, founded in Virginia, 1619.

Bank established: Bank of North America, Philadelphia, 1781.

Birth in America to English parents: Virginia Dare, born Roanoke Island, N.C., 1587.

Botanic garden: Established by John Bartram in Philadelphia, 1728. (Oldest still existing was established in Cambridge, Mass., in 1807.)

Cartoon, colored: "The Yellow Kid," by Richard Outcault, in *New York World*, 1895.

College: Harvard, founded 1636.

College to confer degrees on women: Oberlin (Ohio) College, 1841.

College to establish coeducation: Oberlin (Ohio) College, 1833.

Electrocution of a criminal: William Kemmler in Auburn Prison, Auburn, N.Y., Aug. 6, 1890.

Five and Ten Cents Store: Founded by Frank Woolworth, Utica, N.Y., 1879 (moved to Lancaster, Pa., same year).

Fraternity: Phi Beta Kappa; founded Dec. 5, 1776, at College of William and Mary.

The main heading "Firsts in America" tells you at a glance what the list is about. Events are printed in alphabetical order. They are also in dark print, or **boldface**, so they stand out. What was the first college? What was the first colored cartoon? Both of these firsts are easy to locate in the list.

Now look at a typical chart from an almanac.

Highest recorded temperature

	Place	Date	Degree Fahrenheit	Degree Centigrade
World (Africa)	El Azizia, Libya	Sept. 13, 1922	136	58
North America (U.S.)	Death Valley, Calif.	July 10, 1913	134	57
Asia	Tirat Tsvi, Israel	June 21, 1942	129	54
Australia	Cloncurry, Queensland	Jan. 16, 1889	128	53
Europe	Seville, Spain	Aug. 4, 1881	122	50
South America	Rivadavia, Argentina	Dec. 11, 1905	120	49
Antarctica	Esperanza, Palmer Peninsula	Oct. 20, 1956	58	14

Again, the main heading tells you what the chart is about. The other headings tell you how the chart is arranged. The chart lists the seven highest temperatures ever recorded by area, place and date. The temperature is given in degrees Fahrenheit and Centigrade. As you can see, the place that had the highest temperature was El Aziza, Libya. The place with the lowest temperature was Esperanza, Palmer Peninsula.

A The list below is from the *Information Please Almanac*. Read the list, then answer the questions that follow.

The Names of the Months

January: named after Janus, protector of the gateway to heaven
February: named after Februalia, a time period when sacrifices were made to atone for sins
March: named after Mars, the god of war, presumably signifying that the campaigns interrupted by the winter could be resumed
April: from *aperire*, Latin for "to open" (buds)
May: named after Maia, the goddess of growth of plants
June: from *juvenis*, Latin for "youth"
July: named after Julius Caesar
August: named after Augustus, the first Roman Emperor
September: from *septem*, Latin for "seven"
October: from *octo*, Latin for "eight"
November: from *novem*, Latin for "nine"
December: from *decem*, Latin for "ten"

NOTE: The earliest Latin calendar was a 10-month one; thus September was the seventh month, October, the eighth, etc. July was originally called Quintilis, as the fifth month; August was originally called Sextilis, as the sixth month.

1. What does the list show? ....

2. How many months are in the list? ....

3. How did January get its name? ....

....

4. Is April a good name for that month? Why or why not?

....

....

5. How did December get its name? ....

....

6. Why is September named after the Latin word for "seven"?

....

....

....

7. Who was the first Roman emperor? ....

8. What was the original name for August?

....   ▶

B The chart that follows is from the *Information Please Almanac.* Use the chart to answer the questions.

World's Highest Dams

Name	River, Country or State	Structural height		Gross reservoir capacity		Year completed
		feet	meters	thousands of acre feet	millions of cubic meters	
Rogun	Vakhsh, U.S.S.R.	1066	325	9,404	11,600	UC*
Nurek	Vakhsh, U.S.S.R.	984	300	8,512	10,500	UC*
Grande Dixence	Dixence, Switzerland	935	285	324	400	1962
Inguri	Inguri, U.S.S.R.	892	272	801	1,100	UC
Chicoasén	Grijalva, Mexico	869	265	1,346	1,660	1981
Vaiont	Vaiont, Italy	869	265	137	169	1961
Tehri	Bhagirathi, India	856	261	2,869	3,540	UC*
Kinshau	Tons, India	830	253	1,946	2,400	UC*
Mica	Columbia, Canada	794	242	20,000	24,670	1972

*Uncompleted

1. What does the chart show? ....

....

2. How many dams are on the list? ....

3. How is the list arranged? ....

....

4. Name five facts the chart gives about dams.

....

....

5. What country has the two highest dams? ....

6. In what year were they completed? ....

7. How tall is the Mica dam in Canada?

....

8. What is the name of the dam on the Tons River in India?

....

Using the Contents Section and the Index

Not all almanacs are arranged the same way. Subjects are arranged in different ways. Some have a contents section, and others do not. In some, the index is in the front of the book. In others, the index is in the back. As you have read, the *World Almanac* has two indexes, one in front and one in back.

If you want to find a topic quickly, use the index. The General Index, as you know, is at the front of the *World Almanac. Information Please* has an index at the back.

Like other indexes, an almanac's index lists topics in alphabetical order. Look at the following section of an almanac's index.

Washington (state), 688–89
   Mountains and volcanoes, 456
   See also States of U.S.
Washita River, 470
Wassermann Test, 347
Water:
   Boiling and freezing points, 367
   World supply, 493
Waterfalls, 464–65
Watergate, 121–22, 683
Waterloo, Battle of, 111, 193, 281
Waterways, traffic on, 71, 72
Watt, James, 109, 347, 570
Watt (measure), 364
Watts riots (1966), 121
Watusi, 161, 162
Weapons, 783, 784, 785, 789
Weather and climate, 424–430,
   449–50
   Disastrous storms, 429–30, 450
   Glossary, 428
   Hurricanes, 424, 428, 429–30
   Of U.S. cities, 425–27
   Tornadoes, 428, 430
   Tropical storms, 424
   World extremes, 424, 427

Main topics are in boldface. Some main topics have subtopics. Those are indented. Page numbers after each topic tell you where to find them in the book.

Suppose you want information on storms. If you look under weather and climate, you will see the subtopic **Disastrous Storms**. The page numbers are 429–30 and 450. Does this almanac have facts on waterfalls? Yes, and in this case **Waterfalls** is the main entry in the index.

Notice the second topic under **Washington (state)**. It says *See also* States of U.S. That means that you can find a listing for more information on the state of Washington elsewhere in the index. To locate that listing, you would look under *S* for **States of U.S.**

▶

□ Here is a page from the *Information Please* index. Use it to answer the questions that follow.

1. On what pages will you find information on skyscrapers?

    ....

2. Name two subtopics under **South Pole**.

    ....

3. Under what two subjects is the speed of sound listed?

    ....

4. Under what other topic can you look for information
   on space exploration?

    ....

5. On what page can you find information on football stadiums?

    ....

6. Under what other topic can you look for information on the
   Six-Day War?

    ....

7. What was the Spirit of St. Louis? ....

8. Is Sri Lanka a city, state or country? .... ■

Understanding an Atlas

An atlas is, first of all, a collection of maps. The word *atlas* comes from the name of an ancient Greek giant, whose job it was to hold the world on his shoulders. The first known book of maps had a picture of Atlas on the cover. Later, as others printed their own books of maps, they too put Atlas on the cover. In time, any book of maps was known as an atlas, a practice that goes on today.

The opening sentence of this lesson says that an atlas is *first of all* a collection of maps. Any good atlas has much more than maps. It will have charts and graphs that show the weather in many parts of the world. Other charts and graphs will show where the world's minerals and energy sources are, and who uses them. An atlas will also have facts about where people live and how they are governed. It will tell what languages they speak and what cities they live in. In short, an atlas is an almost endless supply of useful information about the places of the world.

To help you find what you need, an atlas has a contents page and an index. The contents page, located at the front of the book, lists pages on which the maps and other illustrations can be found. The index, usually found at the back of the book, is helpful in finding specific places on a map. For instance, if you want to find Shelby, North Carolina, on a map, you should look first at the index. There you will find an entry something like this:

Shelby, N.C., U.S. **36** G 4

The initials *N.C.* and *U.S.* tell what state and country Shelby is in. (There are five other Shelbys in other states.) The number *36* in boldfaced type tells you that the map is on page 36.

The number 4 and the letter G refer to the letter-number guide across the top and sides of the map. The guide will help you find Shelby quickly. To do so, first look at the top of the map to find the letter G. Then find the 4 on the side of the map. Finally, trace across and down with your fingers until the G and the 4 meet. There you will find Shelby, North Carolina.

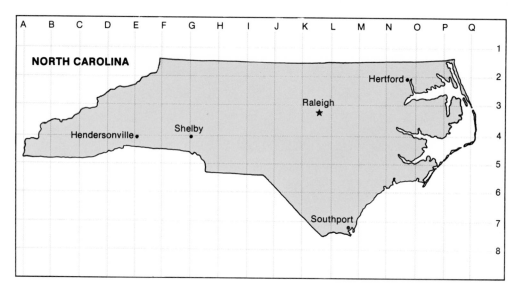

Like any other reference book, an atlas is useful for certain kinds of facts. When you think of maps, think atlas.

Complete each answer in your own words, then check your answers with the key on page 204.

1. An atlas is ....

2. To help find what you need, an atlas will have a

.... and ....

3. Besides maps, an atlas has facts on .... ,

.... and ....

4. If you want to find the location of a specific place, the part of

the atlas you should turn to first is ....

Recognizing Maps in an Atlas

An atlas has many different kinds of maps. Political maps show countries, states and cities. Landform maps show mountains, lowlands, lakes and rivers. Population maps show where people live, and land-use maps tell how people use the land and water.

Below is a map that shows the average amount of rain that falls each year across the United States. Like many other maps, this one has a **key**, which is a small section set apart from the rest of the map that explains the various lines and shadings on the map.

Find Iowa on the map. How many inches of rain fall there each year? Write the answer below.

....

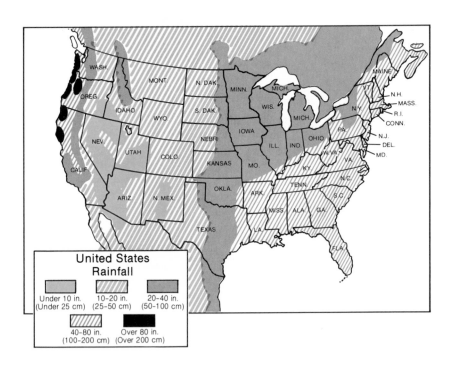

The following map is a population map of South America. It shows where people live on that continent. Look at the key. Most of the centers of people seem to be on the sea-coast or near great rivers. Can you guess why? If you were to look at a landform map and a rainfall map of the same areas, you would see clearly that people live where there is enough rain to grow things and where the land is easy to build on and to travel across.

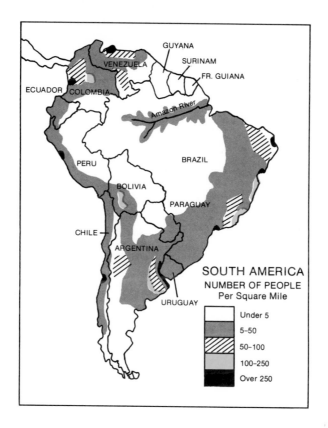

A Use the population map below of the Middle Atlantic states to answer the questions that follow.

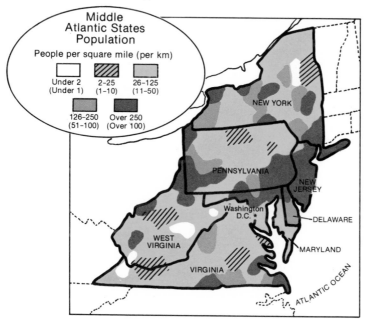

1. How many states make up the Middle Atlantic group?

....   ▶

2. Which is the largest state? ....

3. Which state is the smallest? ....

4. Which state is the farthest north? ....

5. Which state is the farthest south? ....

6. What is the greatest number of people per square mile

   shown by the key? ....

7. How can you tell which areas have between 26 and 125

   people living per square mile? ....

   ....

8. What states seem to have the least populated areas?

   ....

   ....

   ....

9. In which state will you find the area with the least number

   of people per square mile? ....

10. Name four states that are among the most heavily populated.

   ....

   ....

   ....

   ....

More About Maps in an Atlas

Many atlases have resource maps. These show natural resources such as coal, oil and gas, gold, silver, iron ore and so on. Some resource maps include several different kinds of resources, while others show just one kind. Below is a resource map showing major coal fields in the United States. What two kinds of coal does the map show? Write your answers on these lines:

....

....

Does Kansas have any coal fields? Which kind?

....

....

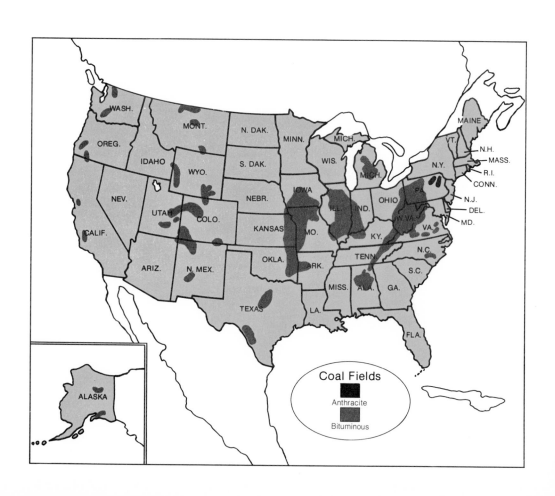

Now look at a resource map that includes several kinds of natural resources. How many different kinds does the map show?

....

Which resource is found in the most states?

....

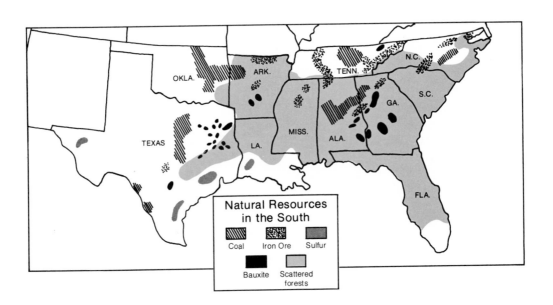

Natural Resources in the South

☐ Put an **X** in the box beside the answer that best completes each statement. Use the resource map below to help you complete the statements.

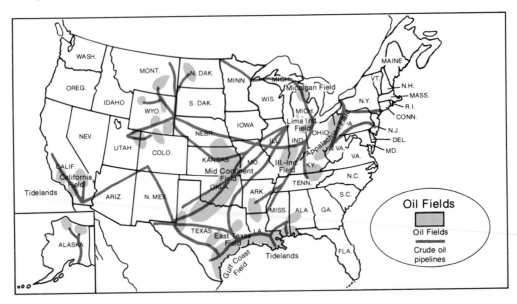

1. The map shows
   - ☐ a. oil fields in the United States.
   - ☐ b. coal and oil fields in the United States.
   - ☐ c. a network of major roads in the United States.

2. The heavy black lines on the map show
   - ☐ a. roads over which tank trucks carry crude oil.
   - ☐ b. the way to coal and gas fields.
   - ☐ c. pipelines that carry crude oil.

3. One large oil field in the south is known as the
   - ☐ a. Appalachian Field.
   - ☐ b. Michigan Field.
   - ☐ c. East Texas Field.

4. Three states that have no oil fields are
   - ☐ a. Washington, Idaho, and Montana.
   - ☐ b. Florida, Georgia, and South Carolina.
   - ☐ c. Kansas, Missouri, and Illinois.

5. Three of the largest oil fields are known as the
   - ☐ a. Mid Continent Field, East Texas Field, Gulf Coast Field.
   - ☐ b. Lima Indiana Field, California Field, Illinois-Indiana Field.
   - ☐ c. Appalachian Field, Colorado Field, Vermont Field.

6. Most of the oil found in the United States is in the
   - ☐ a. Southern states.
   - ☐ b. New England area.
   - ☐ c. Southwest.

■

Reference Skills Achievement Test

I. Library

A. The sections of a library are listed below. Write the letter of the section where you would expect to find each of the following items.

a. Fiction Books
b. Nonfiction Books
c. Children's Room
d. Audiovisual Section
e. Reference
f. Periodicals

.... 1. *Information Please Almanac*

.... 2. *Swan Lake* (record)

.... 3. *Mother Goose Rhymes* (book of poetry)

.... 4. *Seventeen* (magazine)

.... 5. *World Book Encyclopedia*

.... 6. *English Skills* (textbook)

.... 7. *Black Beauty* (novel)

.... 8. *Stories for Children* (book of short stories)

.... 9. "How To Make a Puppet" (slide film)

.... 10. *Washington Post* (newspaper)

B. Circle the source you would check *first* to find the following information.

1. definition of a word   (dictionary, encyclopedia)

2. article in a magazine   (*Readers' Guide*, card catalog)

3. map   (almanac, atlas)

4. addresses   (handbook, directory)

5. list of books   (atlas, bibliography)

6. today's news   (newspaper, yearbook)

7. broad view of a subject   (almanac, encyclopedia)

8. article in the *New York Times* (*New York Times Index*, *New York Times Contents*)

C. Put a check mark (✔) by each statement that is true of the *Readers' Guide to Periodical Literature.*

.... 1. It lists articles in magazines.
.... 2. It lists articles in newspapers.
.... 3. It is a kind of index.
.... 4. It is arranged alphabetically.
.... 5. It contains subject entries.
.... 6. It contains author entries.
.... 7. It tells the page on which an article can be found.
.... 8. It tells whether an article is illustrated.
.... 9. It tells whether an article is well written.
...... 10. It is published once a year.

II. Dictionary

A. Below are six entries from a dictionary. On the line before each entry, write the number of the statement that applies.

.... **pie bald** (pi'bôld), **1** spotted in two colors, especially black and white. **2** a piebald horse. 1 *adj.*, 2 *n.*

.... **bon fire** (bon'fir'), a large fire built outdoors. *n.*

.... **Get tys burg** (get'ez berg'), town in Pennsylvania. An important battle of the Civil War was fought there. *n.*

.... **filch** (filch), steal in small quantities; pilfer: *She filched cookies from the pantry. v.*—**filch'er,** *n.*

.... **Pi cas so** (pi kä'so), **Pablo,** 1881–1973, Spanish painter and sculptor. *n.*

.... **gim let** (gim'let), a small tool with a screw point, for boring holes. *n.*

1. His paintings are very valuable.
2. You would use this to bore a hole.
3. A person who does this could get into trouble.
4. You might find wood in this.
5. Many people visit here.
6. You could describe some ponies this way.

B. In this section, the top group of words is a list of pronunciations for the bottom group of words. To match the pronunciations with the words, write the letters from the top group in the spaces before the words in the bottom group.

a. der   b. klōTH   c. kyü   d. klôŦH   e. fil
f. dir   g. klot   h. ô   i. ō   j. kyür
k. fīl

.... 1. cure   .... 5. clot   .... 9. clothe

.... 2. cloth   .... 6. oh   ....10. file

.... 3. awe   .... 7. dare   ....11. cue

.... 4. dear   .... 8. fill

III. Encyclopedia

A. Underline the word you would use to find each topic below in an encyclopedia.

1. the Great Lakes
2. history of computers
3. rivers in Africa
4. flags of the world
5. Industrial Revolution
6. Roman Empire
7. migration of birds
8. rules of baseball
9. air transportation
10. Sir Isaac Newton

B. The headings below are from an encyclopedia article. Put a check mark (✔) in front of each topic you might expect to find discussed in that article.

The Earth

The Earth's Structure   Seas, Lakes, Rivers
Surface Features   Weather and Climate
Rocks   The Changing Year

.... natural resources   .... mountains
.... the Earth's crust   .... animals and people
.... ocean tides   .... growth of America
.... space exploration   .... railroads
.... the seasons   .... how a river is formed
.... the planets   .... sports

IV. Almanac

A. The following chart is from the *Information Please Almanac.* Read the list, then put a check mark (✔) by the statements that are true.

Calories, Minerals, and Vitamins of Selected Foods

Food and amount	Energy (calories)	Protein (gm)	Fat (gm)	Calcium (mg)	Iron (mg)	Vitamin A (IU)	Vitamin B₁ (thiamin) (mg)	Vitamin B₂ (riboflavin) (mg)	Niacin (mg)	Vitamin C (ascorbic acid) (mg)
Apple, 1 medium, raw	80	—	1	10	.4	120	.04	.03	.1	6
Applesauce, 1 cup, canned, unsweetened	100	—	—	10	1.2	100	.05	.02	.1	2
Bacon, 2 slices, crisp	85	4	8	2	.5	—	.08	.05	.8	—
Banana, 1 medium	100	1	—	10	.8	230	.06	.07	.8	—
Beans, snap green, 1 cup cooked	30	2	—	63	.8	680	.09	.11	.6	12
Beans, red kidney, 1 cup canned	230	15	1	74	4.6	10	.13	.10	1.5	15
Beans, baked, pork and molasses, 1 cup	385	16	12	161	5.9	—	.15	.10	1.3	—
Beef cuts, cooked: Chuck, boned, 3 ounces	245	23	16	10	2.9	30	.04	.18	3.6	—
Hamburger, 3 ounces	235	20	17	9	2.6	30	.07	.17	4.4	—
Rib roast, 3 ounces boned	375	17	33	8	2.2	70	.05	.13	3.1	—
Round, 3 ounces boned	220	24	13	10	3.0	20	.07	.19	4.8	—
Sirloin, 3 ounces boned	330	20	27	9	2.5	50	.05	.15	4.0	—
Beef stew with vegetables, 1 cup	220	16	11	29	2.9	2,400	.15	.17	4.7	17
Beets, 1 cup cooked	55	2	—	24	.9	30	.05	.07	.5	10
Breads: Cracked wheat, average slice	65	2	1	22	.5	—	.08	.06	.8	—
Italian, average slice, enriched	85	3	—	.5	.7	—	.12	.07	1.0	—
Raisin, average slice enriched	65	2	1	18	.6	—	.09	.06	.6	—
Rye (American), average slice	60	2	—	19	.5	—	.07	.05	.7	—
White, average slice enriched	70	2	1	21	.6	—	.10	.06	.8	—
Whole wheat, average slice	65	3	1	24	.8	—	.09	.03	.8	—
Butter, 1 tbsp	100	—	12	3	—	430	—	—	—	—
Cabbage, 1 cup, raw, coarsely shredded	15	1	—	34	.3	90	.04	.04	.2	33
Cake: Sponge, average slice	195	5	4	20	1.1	300	.09	.14	.6	—
Pound, average slice	160	2	10	6	.5	80	.05	.06	.4	—
Candies: Caramels, 1 ounce	115	1	3	42	.4	—	.01	.05	.1	—
Chocolate, milk, 1 ounce	145	2	9	65	.3	80	.02	.10	.1	—
Cantaloupe, 1/2 melon	80	2	—	38	1.1	9,240	.11	.08	1.6	90
Carrot, raw, 1 average size	30	1	—	27	.5	7,930	.04	.04	.4	6
Catsup, 1 tbsp	15	—	—	3	.1	210	.01	.01	.2	2
Cheese: Cheddar, 1 ounce	115	7	9	204	.2	300	.01	.11	—	—
Cottage, creamed, 1 cup	235	28	10	135	.3	370	.05	.37	.3	—
Cottage, uncreamed, 1 cup	125	25	1	46	.3	40	.04	.21	.2	—
Cream cheese, 1 ounce	100	2	10	23	.3	400	—	.06	—	—
Swiss, natural, 1 ounce	105	8	8	272	—	240	.01	.10	—	—
Swiss, process, 1 ounce	95	7	7	219	.2	230	—	.08	—	—
Chicken, broiled, 3 ounces	115	20	3	8	1.4	80	.05	.16	7.4	—

.... 1. The list is arranged by number of calories.

.... 2. Catsup has fifteen calories per tablespoon.

.... 3. There is no protein in an apple.

.... 4. One cup of beef stew has 11 grams of fat.

.... 5. Calories are units of energy.

.... 6. There is no vitamin A in Swiss cheese.

.... 7. One medium banana has the same number of calories as 1 tablespoon of butter.

.... 8. One cup of cabbage has 33 milligrams of vitamin C.

B. The following portion of an index is from the *Information Please Almanac.* Check (✔) each statement that is true about the index.

Virginia, 687–88
   See also States of U.S.
Virgin Islands, British, 285
Virgin Islands, U.S., 115, 692
Virgin Islands National Park, 497
VISTA, 619
Vitamins:
   Content of foods, 87–89
   Dietary allowances, 83–84, 86
   Discoveries, 347
V-J Day (1945), 117, 118
Volcanoes, 449, 456–57, 469
   Famous eruptions, 469
   "Ring of Fire," 456–57
Volcano Islands, 456
Volga River, 463
   Hydroelectric plants on, 435
   Lakes, 462
Volleyball, 848
Volume:
   Formulas for, 366
   Measure of, 360, 361, 362–63,
     366
Volunteers of America, 392
Voskhod flights, 338
Vostok flights, 338
Voting:
   18-year-olds 121, 583
   Plurality and majority, 22
   Presidential elections, 599–607
   Qualification by state, 607
   Rights, 581, 583
   Unusual voting results, 607
   Women's suffrage, 115, 581, 792
Voyager probes, 123, 336, 337
Voyageurs National Park, 497

.... 1. The index is in alphabetical order.

.... 2. The almanac contains information on volcanoes.

.... 3. Facts about volleyball can be found on page 921.

.... 4. There are nine pages on voting in presidential elections.

.... 5. V-J Day took place in 1945.

.... 6. The almanac explains how to measure volume.

.... 7. Some of the Virgin Islands are owned by Spain.

.... 8. Facts about the Virgin Islands National Park are on page 497.

V. Atlas

Use the following rainfall map of Canada to help you answer the questions. Write your answers on the lines provided.

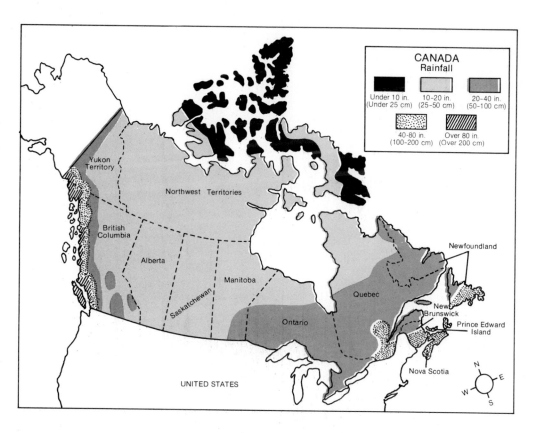

1. In what direction is Canada from the United States?

   ....

2. Provinces and territories in Canada are like states in the United States. How many provinces and territories are there in Canada?

   ....

   ....

3. Which appears to be the largest territory?

   ....

4. How many different areas of rainfall does the map show?

    ....

5. What is the greatest amount of rain that falls on Canada
   in a year?

    ....

6. In what part of the country does the most amount of rain
   fall each year?

    ....

7. How many inches of rain can be expected each year in
   the province of Saskatchewan?

    ....

8. What part of the country seems to be the driest?

    ....

9. About how much rain might you expect to fall each year
   in the driest part?

    ....

Developing Textbook Skills

Recognizing the Parts of a Textbook

Have you ever wondered why a textbook is arranged the way it is? Every book that you read is arranged the way it is for a reason. Each part has a purpose.

The parts of a textbook can be grouped as follows:

1. the binding
2. the opening pages
3. the text
4. reference material

The **binding** is the cover that holds the book together.

The **opening pages** include the title page, copyright page, preface, and contents page.

The **text** is the main body of the book.

Reference materials are found at the end of a book. They are the appendix, glossary, bibliography and index. A textbook may contain all or none of these references. Some may have only an index.

When you get a new textbook, take the time to look at how it is arranged. Read the title. Then turn to the contents page to find out what you will be learning from the book. The table of contents lists the titles of the units and the chapters, and the numbers of the pages on which they begin. Flip through the text pages to see what they look like. Then turn to the back of the book to see what reference materials are there. If you become familiar with all the parts of a textbook, you will be able to make the best use of the book as a learning tool. Your reading and studying will be easier.

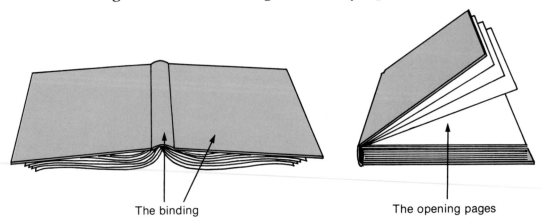

The binding   The opening pages

Now answer the following questions about what you have just read. Write your answers on the blank lines. Then check them against the answer key on page 205.

1. What holds a book together? ....

2. Name two pages included in the opening pages of a book.

....

....

3. What is another name for the text of a book?

....

4. Give two examples of reference materials found in a book.

....

....

5. What parts of a book are sometimes not included?

....

The text

Reference material

Understanding the Opening Pages

The following pages may be included in the opening pages of a textbook. They will usually appear in the order in which they are presented here. Not every book will include all of the pages, however.

The Title Page. The title page is the first important printed page in a book. As you might guess, it features the title of the book. Sometimes there is also a subtitle that adds to or explains the main title.

Following the book's title is the name of the author or authors. If the author has a scholastic title, such as doctor or professor, that is added to his or her name.

Near the bottom of the page is the name of the publisher and the place of publication.

Copyright Page. The copyright page is on the back of the title page. A copyright gives the owner of the book—either the author or the publishing company—all rights to the work. That means that no one else may copy or publish any of the material that is in the book without permission.

Dedication Page. Some authors like to dedicate their books to people who have helped them in their research or writing. They do so on the dedication page. Many textbooks will not have a dedication page.

Preface. The preface is sometimes called a **foreword**. Its purpose is to introduce the author to the reader. Often the author gives his or her reasons for writing the book. The preface may also explain the special features of a book. For many textbooks, prefaces are unnecessary and are not included.

Contents Page. The contents page (or pages) shows the main topics covered in the book and the order in which a book is arranged. It lists the chapters or units of a book with their beginning page numbers.

Introduction. The introduction describes the general subject and plan of the book. It may be written by the author or by someone else who has read the book.

[A] On the blank lines, write the answers to the questions below.

1. What is the first important printed page in a book?

....

2. Where do the name of the publisher and the place of publication appear?

....

3. Why is a copyright important? ....

....

4. What part of a book introduces the author to the reader?

....

5. On what page does an author show thanks to those who

   have been of help? ....

6. What part of a book shows its arrangement?

....

7. What is the main purpose of the preface? ....

....

8. Where is the plan of a book explained? ....

.... ▶

B Design your own title page in the space below. Look at the title page of one of your textbooks to see how the information should be arranged. Use the following information.

AUTHOR: J. A. Lester
BOOK: *Discovering Books*
SUBTITLE: A Handbook for
    Students
JOB TITLE: Professor of English
PUBLISHER: B&W Associates
PLACE: New York

Recognizing Reference Sections

At the end of many textbooks you may find one or more of the following features. They are references to help you use the book. Not every textbook will include all of these features.

Appendix. The word *appendix* comes from a Latin word meaning "something added." An appendix contains material that is related to topics mentioned in the text, but not necessary to have *in* the text. The appendix of a social studies book might have maps. A science book might include a list of inventions, a time line and charts.

Bibliography. Sometimes an author uses other sources to write a book. Often the names of those sources are put together in a list called a bibliography. Another kind of bibliography is a list of suggested books for further reading on a subject.

Glossary. Many subjects use special, technical or hard words. A glossary is a list of those words and their definitions, usually arranged in alphabetical order. The word *glossary,* by the way, comes from the Latin word *glossa,* which means "a hard word that needs to be explained."

Index. The index is the key to a textbook. It tells where information on all the subjects, people and events mentioned can be found in a book. The items in an index are arranged in alphabetical order.

☐ Complete a glossary of textbook terms by filling in the blanks below. You will have to write either a term or its definition. Remember that the words in a glossary are in alphabetical order.

.... : a reference that includes material related to the text but not necessary to it

.... : a list of sources used by the author, or a list of books for suggested reading ▶

Binding: ....

....

Body: ....

....

Contents Page: ....

....

....

.... : a page in the opening pages of a book
that gives the copyright date

Dedication Page: ....

....

Glossary: ....

....

....

Index: ....

....

....

.... : the page that describes the general subject and plan of the book

Preface: ....

....

.... : the page that gives the book's title, its author and publication information   ■

Using a Globe

A globe is the most accurate model of the earth. Because the earth is nearly round, a globe is round. For that reason, a globe gives a truer picture of the earth than a flat world map does. Indeed, it is impossible to show the distances, directions and areas of the round world accurately on a flat map. A globe, though, deals with those elements much more accurately. Compare the flat-map picture of North and South America below with the picture of a globe showing the same areas of the world and you will see the difference clearly.

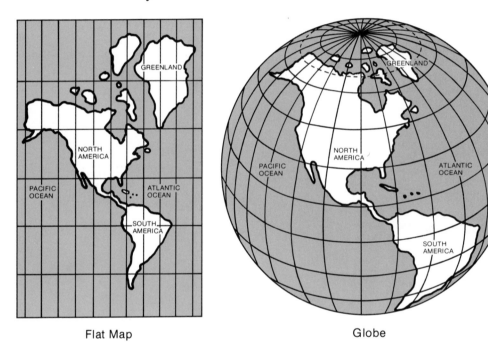

Flat Map   Globe

Notice especially that the continent of Greenland appears out-of-shape and enlarged on the flat map.

Globes, then, have several advantages over flat maps. One is that a globe always shows the true location of a place on the earth's surface. Places are also shown in their correct relative size on a globe. A second advantage is that distances measured on a globe are always accurate.

Flat maps have one important advantage, though. They are easier to use and store. Can you imagine, for example, trying to use a globe as a road map?

Complete each sentence in your own words. Then check your answers with the answer key on page 205.

1. It is impossible to show the earth accurately on a map because a map is ....

2. The truest picture of the earth is shown on a ....

3. Two advantages a globe has over a flat map are .... and ....

4. One advantage of flat world maps over a globe is ....

This is not a globe; this is a photograph of Earth taken from the Apollo 17 spacecraft. Despite the heavy cloud cover, the coastline of Africa is visible in the center of the planet. The picture is remarkable, but a globe would be more useful for finding parts of the world and the distances that separate them.

Finding Direction on a Globe

Because a globe is a round model of the earth, you can see only one-half of the globe at a time. The half you see is called a **hemisphere**. The word comes from two ancient Greek words: *hemi,* meaning "half," and *sphere,* meaning "shaped like a ball."

At the top of the globe is the North Pole. At the bottom is the South Pole. An imaginary line called the **equator** runs around the center of the globe. North and south directions are calculated by using the equator as a starting point.

Look at the picture of the earth below. It is in the shape of a stretched out globe, so you can see both the Eastern and Western Hemispheres at once. Notice how all of North America lies north of the equator. Africa lies partly north of the equator and partly to the south. All the lands and waters north of the equator are in the **Northern Hemisphere**. All lands and waters south of the equator are in the **Southern Hemisphere**.

There is one other important imaginary line on the globe. It is called the **prime meridian**. The word *prime* means "first," and *meridian* comes from an old Latin word that means "midday," or "noon." The prime meridian runs halfway around the globe, from the North Pole, through the town of Greenwich, England, and on to the South Pole. All east and west directions are calculated by using the prime meridian as a starting point.

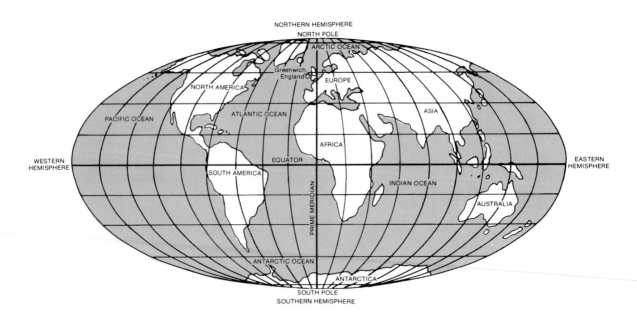

In the picture of the earth on the left, notice that North and South America are west of the prime meridian. They are in the **Western Hemisphere**. And since all of Asia is east of the prime meridian, that continent lies in the **Eastern Hemisphere**.

☐ Use the pictures of the earth on page 118 to complete the sentences that follow.

1. The imaginary line that divides the globe into the Northern

   and Southern Hemispheres is called the ....

2. The imaginary line that divides the globe into the Eastern

   and Western Hemispheres is called the ....

   ....

3. Africa is partly in the .... Hemisphere

   and partly in the .... Hemisphere.

4. The Arctic Ocean is in the .... Hemisphere.

5. Two continents that are in both the Northern and the

   Southern Hemispheres are .... and

   ....

6. The continent shown as extending farthest south is

   ....

7. The town you live in is in the ....

   Hemisphere.   ▶

8. The globe shows the .... , ... , ... , and .... Oceans.

9. The ocean that lies between North America and Europe is the .... Ocean.

10. In going from Africa to Europe, you would travel in a .... direction.

11. In going from North America to Europe, you would travel from .... to ....

12. To travel from Greenwich, England, to Antarctica, you would cross the .... as you moved from the .... Hemisphere to the .... Hemisphere.

13. Most of the land areas on the globe are located in the .... Hemisphere.

Finding Distances on a Globe

One advantage of a globe, as you have learned, is that distances on one are always accurate. That is because the globe is a true model of the earth.

Like any model, the globe is a scaled-down copy of the real thing. (After all, where would you put a full-size model!)

Scaling is a way of reducing size to create a model that has the same appearance as the original. For example, using a scale of one inch to one foot, a model of a seventy-foot boat would be seventy inches long.

Some globes show a scale also. On many globes used in schools the scale is as follows: one inch on the globe equals 500 miles on the earth's surface. Therefore, cities that are three inches apart on the globe are 1,500 miles apart (3 x 500 = 1,500) on the earth. Suppose you measured one and one-half inches between two other cities on the same globe. How far apart would they be? Write your answer here:

....

If you said 750 miles, you are right.

Even if a globe doesn't show a scale, you can easily measure distance. But first you need to know that the globe has lines other than the equator and the prime meridian. Lines on the globe that run from east to west are called parallels, or **latitude** lines. Lines that run from north to south are called meridians, or **longitude** lines. Both kinds of lines are used in taking directions and measuring distances. Here is what latitude and longitude lines look like on the globe.

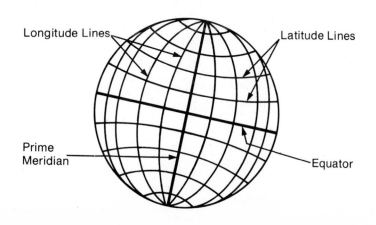

Longitude Lines

Latitude Lines

Prime Meridian

Equator

Latitude and longitude lines are measured in degrees rather than in miles. One degree of latitude on the globe equals 70 miles on the earth's surface. To find the globe's scale, follow these four simple steps.

1. Measure with a ruler the distance in inches along the prime meridian from the equator to the next latitude line north or south.

2. Read the number of degrees represented by this latitude line. The number of degrees will be printed on or near the prime meridian.

3. Multiply the number of degrees of latitude by 70. This tells you how many miles there are from one latitude line to the next on your globe.

4. Divide the total miles from step 3 by the total inches from step 1. This tells you how many miles there are in each inch on your globe.

For instance, if there are two inches between the equator and the next latitude line along the prime meridian, and each line represents ten degrees, then the globe's scale is one inch equals 350 miles. (10 × 70 = 700, 700 – 2 = 350)

A Put an X in the box beside the answer that best completes each statement.

1. One advantage of a globe is that
   ☐ a. it is always easier to use than a flat map.
   ☐ b. distances on a globe are always accurate.
   ☐ c. a globe shows a scale.

2. On many globes used in schools, the scale is
   ☐ a. one inch equals 500 feet.
   ☐ b. one mile equals 500 miles.
   ☐ c. one inch equals 500 miles.

3. A globe is a
   □ a. picture of the earth.
   □ b. kind of scale.
   □ c. scaled-down model of the earth.

4. Lines on a globe that run from east to west are
   □ a. latitude lines.
   □ b. longitude lines.
   □ c. prime meridians.

5. Lines on a globe that run from north to south are
   □ a. latitude lines.
   □ b. longitude lines.
   □ c. equators.

B Write your answers on the blank lines.

1. You have a globe on which the scale is one inch equals 500 miles. Two cities measure six inches apart. How far apart are the cities on the earth's surface?

   ....

2. Every degree of latitude on a globe is equal to 70 miles on the earth's surface. If you measure 10 degrees of latitude in one inch on the prime meridian, what is the scale of the globe?

   ....

3. There are 90 degrees of latitude between the equator and the North Pole. How many miles on the earth's surface are there between those two points?

   ....

Using Illustrations

Illustrations are a useful addition to any textbook. They help to explain what the text is about. Sometimes you can learn facts not found in the text. The kinds of illustrations that you are likely to find in a textbook are photographs, drawings, diagrams, tables and graphs.

Photographs and drawings are the most common. **Photographs**, of course, are pictures taken by a camera. **Drawings** are done by an artist. An artist does not always see the way a camera "sees." As a result, a drawing of an object may look quite different from a photograph of that object.

Diagrams are also drawings. A **diagram** shows the parts of something—an airplane or a car, for example. Science texts use many diagrams. So do books that teach how to build something.

The aim of a **table** is to give facts in a clear, easy-to-read manner. Tables often take the form of lists. For instance, a table might list the world's tallest mountains, their heights, and where they are located.

A **graph** can show the same information as a table, but graphs use fewer words and numbers. Instead, graphs use lines and shapes such as circles, rectangles, triangles and curves. Graphs usually compare sets of facts. The number of students enrolled in your school last year and this year can be shown on a graph.

Now read the following questions. Write your answers on the blank lines, then check them against the answer key on page 205.

1. Why are illustrations useful? ....

....

2. Where are you likely to find a diagram? ....

....

3. Give an example of something that might be diagramed.

....

4. If you wanted to show the number of people who attended the class play on each of three nights, which kind of illustration would you use? Why?

....

....

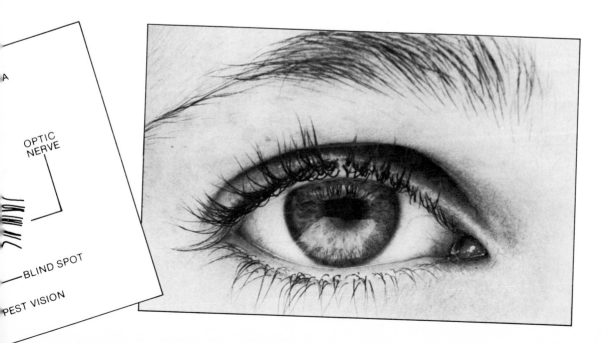

OPTIC
NERVE

—BLIND SPOT

PEST VISION

A

Using Photographs, Drawings and Diagrams

You have probably heard the saying "one picture is worth a thousand words." Sometimes you can learn more by looking at a picture than you can from reading several paragraphs in a textbook.

Some pictures, like the one below, help to explain ideas in the text.

As long ago as the Middle Ages, people wanted to fly in balloons. The English scholar Roger Bacon thought that people might fly if they jumped from high places while wearing globes of thin copper. Luckily, his idea was never tested. In 1783, the Mongolfier brothers of France launched the first balloon to carry a person. That flight lasted about four minutes. Today, hot-air ballooning is quite popular. There are ballooning clubs that organize races and shows, and some people even take cross-country trips in balloons.

The text tells about the history of ballooning, but to get a good idea of what balloons look like, a picture can't be beat.

Drawings are often used instead of photographs. They can illustrate ideas that would be difficult or impossible to photograph, such as scenes from the past. Look at the drawing that follows, for example.

The Battle of Gettysburg was one of the most terrible of the Civil War. Over 3,000 Union soldiers were killed and 20,000 were wounded or missing in action. Confederate losses were also heavy—4,000 men were killed, and 24,000 were wounded or missing in action.

The text gives facts about the battle. The drawing brings those facts to life. Keep in mind that a drawing is not always as true-to-life as a photograph. It is an artist's idea of what something looks like.

Sometimes a diagram is used to explain an idea in a textbook. The diagram on the right shows how to lay out a pattern for a stuffed animal. It would be very difficult to explain this process in words.

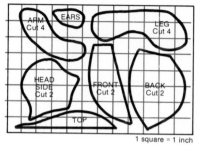

A Read the following text and study the diagram. Then answer the questions.

Here is how a window air conditioner works. A special refrigerant is poured into and passed through a compressor, which raises the pressure of the refrigerant, and then through condenser coils which carry the liquid. Then a condenser fan cools the gas enough to make it turn into a liquid. That causes it to release heat. From the condenser, the refrigerant goes through the evaporator coils. There it evaporates into a gas. That causes it to absorb heat from the room air. These changes occur over and over, and as the air is cooled, it is blown by fans into the room to cool the room. Any moisture that condenses and drips from the evaporator coils is caught in the drip pan.

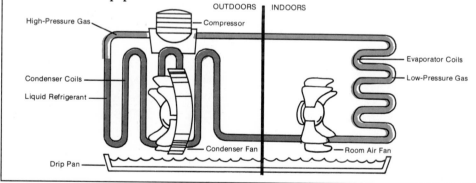

1. What is the purpose of the diagram? ....

....

2. What does the diagram show? ....

....

3. How many parts are shown in the diagram? ....
Underline each of those parts in the text.

▶

4. What, finally, do the text and the diagram combine to tell you?

....

....

....

....

B Read the textbook passage below. Tell whether you think it should be illustrated by a photograph, a drawing or a diagram, and explain your choice.

There are thousands of kinds of ants. They are scattered far and wide over the world. The pictures show a few of the many kinds found in the United States.

....

....

....

....

....

....

....

Tables and Graphs

A table is one way to organize information. Study the facts in this table. Begin by reading the title of the table. Then read the headings above each column. After you have done that, read the facts in each column.

TABLE 1
**RECORD OF AVERAGE
TEMPERATURES, FAHRENHEIT**

Month	Temperature
January	24° F
February	27° F
March	36° F
April	45° F
May	56° F
June	68° F
July	72° F
August	75° F
September	68° F

The table lists temperatures for nine months, from January through September. The hottest month was August. The coldest month was January. Can you find the two months that had the same average temperature? The table shows that June and September both had an average temperature of 68 degrees Fahrenheit.

Another way to organize information is by using a graph. As you can see by the following illustration, a graph can be used to show the same types of information that a table can show.

**RECORD OF AVERAGE TEMPERATURES
IN DEGREES FAHRENHEIT**

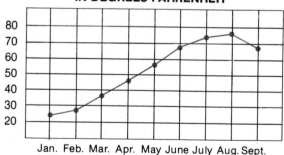

Jan. Feb. Mar. Apr. May June July Aug. Sept.

▶

The graph shows the information in a direct manner that is easy to read. You can see at a glance that the temperature rose through August and dropped in September. You can also see that it did not rise above eighty degrees Fahrenheit. In this case, both the table and the graph made the facts clear. A paragraph filled with the same facts might have been harder to understand. The graph on the previous page is a **line graph**. There are also other kinds of graphs.

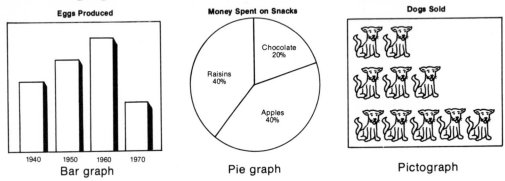

Bar graph

Pie graph

Pictograph

A **bar graph** is used to compare sets of figures. Pie graphs are used to show the parts of a whole—"slices" of the pie stand for parts of a fixed or total amount. A pictograph is somewhat like a bar graph, except it uses pictures instead of bars.

[A] Study the table below. Then answer the questions that follow.

TABLE 2
CURRENT BOOK SUPPLY

Adventure	30
Autobiography	5
Biography	10
Hobby	5
Mystery	25
Sports	25

1. What does the table show? ....

....

2. In what order are the book types arranged?

....

3. Which type has the most books? ....

4. What might be the headings for the two columns?

....

B The same information can be shown on a graph.
Complete the graph below.

CURRENT BOOK SUPPLY

Types of Books	Number of Books
Autobiography	
Biography	
Hobby	□
Sports	□ □ □ □ □
Mystery	
Adventure	□ □ □ □ □ □

□ = 5 Books

C Look at the graph that follows and answer the questions
below it.

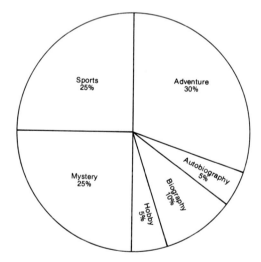

1. What kind of graph is it? ....

2. What does the graph show? ....

3. How does the graph show the amounts of books?

....

Reading a Math Textbook

You already know that you must read in a certain way when you are reading any textbook. You need to read slowly and carefully in order to understand the new concepts. Reading a math textbook takes special effort and attention. You may take twice as long to read a page in a math text as you would to read a page in a social studies text, for instance.

One reason for reading math slowly is that you must learn to read in a different language. Math uses special words and symbols. It takes time to learn this different language.

Also, you must realize that the words and symbols stand for ideas. You need to understand each new idea before you move on to the next one. That is why reading every word in a math textbook is important. If you miss a word, or if you are not sure of the meaning of a word, you may find it hard to understand the whole lesson.

Learning math is a step-by-step process, like building a house. If the foundation is weak, the whole house may collapse. In math, each new idea you learn is based on something you learned earlier.

Math reading takes time, but it is something anyone can learn to do well. The way to learn is to practice slow, careful and thoughtful reading habits.

The statements below refer to what you have just read. Complete each statement by circling the best answer. Be sure to check your answers against the key on page 205.

1. Math reading is different from other reading because
   a. it uses special symbols, words and numbers.
   b. math textbooks are poorly written.
   c. there are a lot of words on a page.

2. It is important to understand each step in math because
   a. one step may collapse.
   b. earlier steps depend on later steps.
   c. each new idea is based on what you learned before.

3. In math reading
   a. every word is important.
   b. you can skip words and still get the meaning.
   c. the faster you read, the better.

4. Words, symbols and numbers in math
   a. are confusing.
   b. are like those in other subjects.
   c. stand for ideas.

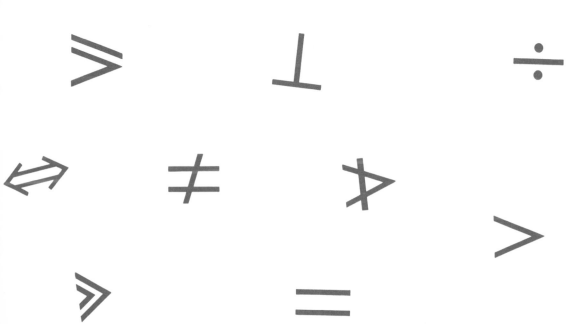

Understanding Math Language

As you know, math has its own special language. You must learn the meanings of the words, symbols and numbers used in that language to grasp the new ideas.

Read the sentences below, for instance.

> What is the language of multiplication? The *multiplicand* is the number to be multiplied. The *multiplier* is the number that does the multiplying. When you multiply, the result is the *product*. The sign for multiplying is ×.

$$
\begin{array}{rl}
3 & \text{multiplicand} \\
\underline{\times 2} & \text{multiplier} \\
6 & \text{product}
\end{array}
$$

You learned several new words. Two of these—*multiplicand* and *multiplier*—are seldom used outside of math. The third word—*product*—has a special meaning when used in math. Besides learning the meaning of these new words you must also learn what the symbol × stands for. The author assumes you know what it means to multiply.

Because they are important, new words and symbols are carefully explained in the text. Notice that the new words are in dark type, or **boldface**. This technique is often used in math books to make key words stand out.

Math books nearly always give examples or illustrations to make meanings clear. Study them carefully.

Sometimes an author may assume you know the meaning of a word. If a word is not explained in the text and you are uncertain of its meaning, do not skip over it. Remember, every word in math reading is important.

Here are some tips for dealing with unexplained words:

- Read on in the text a short way beyond the word in question. Look for examples elsewhere on the page that may explain the word. Then go back and see if the meaning is clear.

- Look for a glossary at the back of the book. It may give the definition of the word.

- Look in the index at the back of the book. If the word is explained elsewhere in the book, the index will tell you where to find the explanation.

- Look the word up in a dictionary.

- Think about the word. Is it like any other word you know? For instance, the word *addition* has the word *add* in it. Knowing that, you can figure out that addition has something to do with adding.

- If you are unable to figure out the meaning of a word, ask your teacher for help.

☐ Read the following page from a math textbook. Then put an **X** in the box beside the answer that best completes each statement.

What Is One Quarter?

The word *quarter* comes from the Latin word *quarto,* meaning four. The word *quarter* now means one-fourth, or one of four parts that are all the same size.

If you cut one-half of an object in half, you will have two quarters of that object.

Cut a circle into halves.

Then cut each half in half.

Each of the parts is one quarter, or one-fourth, of the circle.

Suppose you had 12 stars.

If you divided them in half, you would have six stars in each group. If you divided each half in half, you would have three stars in each group. Each group of three stars is one-fourth of the whole, or one quarter.

one quarter = one-fourth = 1/4

▶

1. The word *quarter* means
   ☐ a. part of a circle.
   ☐ b. one-fourth of something.
   ☐ c. the same size.

2. The text assumes you know the meaning of the word
   ☐ a. circle.
   ☐ b. square.
   ☐ c. quarter.

3. If you did not know the meaning of the word *half*, you could look in
   ☐ a. the glossary.
   ☐ b. the index.
   ☐ c. both the glossary and the index.

4. To make the meaning clear, the text uses
   ☐ a. maps.
   ☐ b. letters.
   ☐ c. illustrations.

5. The symbol = stands for
   ☐ a. equal to.
   ☐ b. less than.
   ☐ c. more than.

6. If you divided a square into quarters you would have
   ☐ a. two equal parts.
   ☐ b. four equal parts.
   ☐ c. five equal parts.

How to Read a Math Problem

Many students are frightened by word problems in math. They do require some thought. But often they sound more difficult than they are.

The key to success in doing math problems is careful reading. Here are some tips to help you:

- Read exactly what the author has written. Do not skip words, or supply words that are not there.

- Do not confuse words or symbols that are alike (*ten* and *tenth*, or $<$ and $>$, for example).

- Math words and symbols stand for ideas. Think about those ideas as you read.

- Make sure you attach the right ideas to the words you are reading. (Do not read *add* and think *subtract*, for example.)

- Picture the problem in your mind or draw a picture to make the problem clear.

Now apply those tips to the following problem.

Bob's yard is shaped like a square. Each of the four sides measures 20 feet. He wants to build a fence around three of the sides. How many feet of fencing should he buy?

First read the problem carefully. The author assumes you know the meaning of the word *square*. If you do not, read further in the problem. It explains that a square has four sides, and that the sides are of equal length, in this case 20 feet.

Your first step would be to draw a picture of the problem.

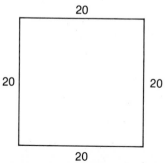

▶

If Bob wants to build a fence around three sides, you know that you must add three of the sides together to get the total number of feet. You could set up the problem like this:

$$20 + 20 + 20 = 60$$

Another way to do the problem is to multiply, like this:

$$20 \times 3 = 60$$

Bob needs 60 feet of fence for his yard.

A Study the following information. Then put an **X** in the box beside the best answer to each question.

TABLE OF EQUIVALENT WEIGHTS AND MEASURES

3 teaspoons = 1 tablespoon	2 cups = 1 pint
1½ teaspoons = ½ tablespoon	4 cups (2 pints) = 1 quart
4 tablespoons = ¼ cup	4 quarts (liquid) = 1 gallon
5 tablespoons	8 quarts (dry) = 1 peck
+ 1 teaspoon = 1/3 cup	4 pecks = 1 bushel
8 tablespoons = ½ cup	1 fluid ounce = 2 tablespoons
10 tablespoons	5 fluid ounces = 1 cup
+ 2 teaspoons = 2/3 cup	32 fluid ounces = 1 quart
16 tablespoons = 1 cup	25 fluid ounces = 1 fifth (of gallon)

1. What does the word *equivalent* mean?
   - ☐ a. Liquid
   - ☐ b. Dry
   - ☐ c. Equal

2. What information does the table give?
   - ☐ a. Weights of tables
   - ☐ b. Equal weights and measures
   - ☐ c. Measurements

3. How many tablespoons are in ½ cup?
   - ☐ a. 8
   - ☐ b. 4
   - ☐ c. 2

4. How many pints are in 4 cups?
   - ☐ a. 2
   - ☐ b. 4
   - ☐ c. 6

5. Which is larger, a gallon or a quart? How do you know?

....

....

B Now read the following word problem. Then put an **X** in the box beside the response that best answers each question.

> Carol needs a quart of milk for a recipe. She has only 1 pint. How many more cups of milk does she need?

1. Which process do you use to arrive at the answer?
   - ☐ a. Addition
   - ☐ b. Subtraction
   - ☐ c. Multiplication

2. What information do you need from the table?
   - ☐ a. 4 cups (2 pints) = 1 quart
   - ☐ b. 4 quarts = 1 gallon
   - ☐ c. 4 tablespoons = ¼ cup

3. What is the answer to the problem?
   - ☐ a. 2
   - ☐ b. ½
   - ☐ c. 4

Learning How to Study

Do you know how to make the most of your study time? Many students need some help in learning how to use their time wisely.

Here are some suggestions to help you develop better study habits:

- Plan to study every day. Make a schedule that allows study time for each subject.

- Keep a record of your homework assignments. Plan ahead so that you have enough time to complete each assignment on time.

- Put any extra time to good use by using it for study or research. Those extra minutes can really add up.

- Choose a good place to study. Make sure it is comfortable, quiet and well lighted so that you can concentrate.

- Learn how to adjust your reading speed to the task at hand. Sometimes you may want to read quickly to get a general idea of the material. At other times you may need to read more slowly to remember facts.

- Learn how to write summaries, or short statements of important facts on some subject.

- Prepare for class. Review your summaries. Make sure you have the supplies you will need—notebook, pencils, textbooks and so on.

- Prepare for tests. Do not try to cram all the material into your head the night before a test. Set aside time at least a week before the test for review. Ask yourself questions about the subject and check your answers. It may sometimes be helpful to study with a friend so that you can test each other.

Now answer these questions about what you have just read. Write your answers on the blank lines. Then check them against the answer key on page 205.

1. Why should you make a schedule? ....

....

2. Why should you record homework assignments?

....

....

3. What are summaries? ....

....

4. Should you always read everything at the same speed? Why or why not?

....

....

5. When is a good time to begin studying for a test?

....

Budgeting Your Time

The secret to using time wisely is budgeting. Just as you budget the money you spend, you should budget your time. A good way to do this is to set up a schedule of your activities. Of course, you do not need to schedule every second. But you should set aside blocks of time for important activities, and that includes time to study each of your subjects every day.

Here is an example of how you might schedule your after-school time:

> 3:30 pm - get out of school
> 3:45 pm - Glee Club
> 5:00 pm - arrive home
> 5:15 pm - study science
> 6:00 pm - read chapter 12, history
> 6:30 pm - eat dinner
> 7:15 pm - study for math test
> 8:00 pm - read chapter of novel for English class
> 9:00 pm - go to bed

Try to stick to your schedule. If you don't finish a subject in the time allowed, go on to the next subject. You can return to the unfinished work later.

Once you have learned how to prepare a daily schedule like the one above, you can make a weekly schedule. A weekly schedule is useful for planning long-range assignments, such as a research paper, a book report or studying for a test.

If you follow your schedule, you will not feel rushed to complete an assignment at the last minute. And spacing your study time over a period of days will make it easier to remember the material for a test.

Another useful schedule is a record of homework assignments. Record when the assignment is due and

estimate the amount of time it will take. Then make sure
you allow enough time on your weekly schedule to complete
the assignment on time.

A Here is a weekly schedule to help you organize your
time after school. Under each day of the school week are
five blocks. Fill in each block with an after-school activity,
starting tomorrow. After S write the time you will start
the activity. After F write the time you will finish that
activity. Try to schedule time to study each of your subjects
every day.

AFTER-SCHOOL SCHEDULE

Monday	Tuesday	Wednesday	Thursday	Friday
S: _____ F: _____	S: _____ F: _____	S: _____ F: _____	S: _____ F: _____	S: _____ F: _____
S: _____ F: _____	S: _____ F: _____	S: _____ F: _____	S: _____ F: _____	S: _____ F: _____
S: _____ F: _____	S: _____ F: _____	S: _____ F: _____	S: _____ F: _____	S: _____ F: _____
S: _____ F: _____	S: _____ F: _____	S: _____ F: _____	S: _____ F: _____	S: _____ F: _____

▶

B Here is a homework record sheet. Each time you are given an assignment, fill in each column with the information called for. Under *Time Needed*, write the amount of time you think you will need to complete the assignment. Be sure you allow for this time on your weekly schedule. You can easily make homework records like this in a notebook.

HOMEWORK RECORD

Class	Due Date	Homework	Time Needed

Reading Skills: Skimming and Study-Reading

Look at the list of reading materials below. Would you read each of them in the same way?

1. Mystery story
2. Magazine article
3. Science textbook

You would probably read the mystery story quickly, because you would want to find out "whodunit." You might just read parts of a newspaper article to get a general idea of what it is about. When reading the science textbook, you would read slowly and carefully to learn new facts and ideas.

It is not necessary to read everything carefully. Learning how to adjust your rate of reading to suit your purpose can help you make better use of your time.

Sometimes you may want to **scan** the material. When you scan, you do not read every word. You look quickly over the material to find a specific fact. For example, you might scan a dictionary page to find a specific word, or a page in a telephone book to find a name and number.

Skimming is reading very quickly to pick out the main ideas. When you skim, you should read as quickly as you can without missing the main points. Skimming is a good way to cover a lot of material in a short period of time. It is often appropriate for reading newspapers and magazines.

Study-reading is slow and careful reading. When you study-read, you read more slowly than you normally do, stopping from time to time to think about what you have read. Your aim is to understand what you have read. You should study-read when you read a textbook or other material that you want to understand completely.

[A] Read the statements that follow. Write *true* in front of a statement that is true, and *false* in front of a statement that is false.

.... 1. When you read to remember facts and ideas, you should skim the material.

.... 2. Good readers always read quickly.

▶

.... 3. Scanning is looking quickly over material to find a specific fact.

.... 4. Study-reading is done at your normal reading rate.

.... 5. Skimming is reading very quickly to pick out main ideas.

.... 6. You should read everything carefully.

B Read the question below. Then scan the passage that follows to find the answer. Write your answer on the blank line.

What is the speed of sound?

....

Sound waves are caused by air molecules that move back and forth, or vibrate. The waves move through the air at a speed of about 1,080 feet (330 meters) per second. We cannot feel most sound waves because their vibrations are not strong enough. But they do make our eardrums vibrate, and that causes us to hear the sound.

C Now skim the passage to find the answer to the question below. Write your answer on the blank line.

What is the paragraph mainly about?

....

D Finally, study-read the passage to find the answers to these questions.

1. What causes sound waves? ....

....

2. Why are we unable to feel most sound waves? ....

....

3. What causes us to hear a sound? ....

.... ■

Textbook Skills Achievement Test

I. Parts of a Textbook

Put an **X** in the box beside the answer that best completes each statement below.

1. The part of a book that holds it together is the
   - ☐ a. binding.
   - ☐ b. title page.
   - ☐ c. text.

2. A copyright is important because it
   - ☐ a. shows who published the book.
   - ☐ b. protects the rights of the owner.
   - ☐ c. protects the rights of the reader.

3. An author shows appreciation in the
   - ☐ a. glossary.
   - ☐ b. introduction.
   - ☐ c. dedication.

4. The part of a book that tells on what pages the subjects, people and events mentioned in the book can be found is the
   - ☐ a. appendix.
   - ☐ b. index.
   - ☐ c. glossary.

5. Maps at the back of a social studies book are part of the
   - ☐ a. index.
   - ☐ b. appendix.
   - ☐ c. bibliography.

6. A list of difficult words and their definitions found in the back of a textbook is a
   - ☐ a. bibliography.
   - ☐ b. preface.
   - ☐ c. glossary.

7. The part of a book that shows how the book is arranged is the
   - ☐ a. contents page.
   - ☐ b. title page.
   - ☐ c. index.

8. The publisher and place of publication are found on the
  □ a. binding.
  □ b. copyright page.
  □ c. title page.

9. The general subject and plan of the book is described in the
  □ a. appendix.
  □ b. title page.
  □ c. introduction.

10. The appendix, glossary, bibliography and index are called
  □ a. text.
  □ b. reference sections.
  □ c. opening pages.

II. Globe

A. Two views of a globe are pictured below. Label the parts by writing the correct names on the blank lines.

....

....

....

.... Hemisphere   .... Hemisphere

B. Put an **X** in the box beside the answer that best completes each statement.

1. A flat world map is
  □ a. more accurate than a globe.
  □ b. less accurate than a globe.
  □ c. neither more nor less accurate than a globe.

2. *Hemi* in the word *hemisphere* means
  □ a. round.
  □ b. half.
  □ c. all.

3. The United States lies in the
   - ☐ a. Northern and Southern Hemispheres.
   - ☐ b. Eastern and Western Hemispheres.
   - ☐ c. Western and Northern Hemispheres.

4. Lines that run from east to west on a globe are
   - ☐ a. latitude lines.
   - ☐ b. longitude lines.
   - ☐ c. meridians.

5. One inch on a globe's scale equals 500 miles. If on that globe two cities are four inches apart, how far apart are the cities on the surface of the earth?
   - ☐ a. 20 miles
   - ☐ b. 200 miles
   - ☐ c. 2,000 miles

III. Illustrations

A. Use the table to answer the questions that follow. Put an X in the box beside the correct answer.

TABLE 3
Record of Average Summer Highway Speeds in Miles per Hour

Month	Speed
June	55 MPH
July	50 MPH
August	60 MPH

1. If the speed limit is 55 miles per hour, in what month did the average speed exceed the speed limit?
   - ☐ a. June
   - ☐ b. July
   - ☐ c. August

2. In what month was the average speed under the 55-mile-per-hour speed limit?
   - ☐ a. June
   - ☐ b. July
   - ☐ c. August

3. How did the average speed for all three months combined compare to the speed limit?
   - ☐ a. The average was over the speed limit.
   - ☐ b. The average was under the speed limit.
   - ☐ c. The average was right on the speed speed limit.

B. On the line graph below, the speeds for June and July are provided for you. Refer to the table on page 150 to find the average speed for August. Then complete the line of the graph by connecting July at 50 MPH to August at 60 MPH.

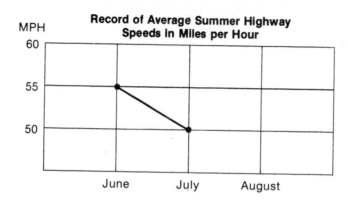

C. Write *T* before each statement that is true, and *F* before each false statement.

.... 1. A table is not a way to organize information.

.... 2. A graph can often show the same types of information that a table can show.

.... 3. The purpose of tables and graphs is to make information clear.

.... 4. A bar graph is used to compare sets of figures.

.... 5. A pie graph is somewhat like a bar graph, except it uses slices of the pie to compare sets of figures.

.... 6. A table and a graph are really no different.

.... 7. Pictographs use pictures to stand for figures or quantities.

.... 8. A pie graph uses slices of the pie to stand for parts of a whole.

IV. Math Textbook

Read this page from a math textbook. Then put an **X** in the box beside the answer that best completes each statement that follows.

STANDARD MEASURES

When you talk about the length of something, you are talking about its measurement. Suppose you have a board that is three feet long, for example. Most people would know what you mean by the measurement "three feet." A foot is a **standard unit of measurement**. It is agreed upon and used by a large number of people.

Some other standard units used by people in measuring are the **inch**, the **yard**, and the **mile**.

12 inches = 1 foot
3 feet = 1 yard
5,280 feet = 1,760 yards = 1 mile

---

1. The word *standard* means
   □ a. alike.
   □ b. according to a rule.
   □ c. not usual.

2. Standard units of measurement are needed so that
   □ a. all measurements are equal.
   □ b. something can be measured.
   □ c. everyone understands a measurement.

3. To find how many inches are in one mile you would
   □ a. add.
   □ b. subtract.
   □ c. multiply.

4. In 4 yards there are
   □ a. 8 feet.
   □ b. 10 feet.
   □ c. 12 feet.

5. Sarah wants to build a square birdhouse. For the sides of the house, she has four boards of equal length. Placed end to end, they measure four feet. When she has built her birdhouse, each side will measure

☐ a. two feet.
☐ b. one foot.
☐ c. four feet.

V. How To Study

A. Put a check mark (✔) by each statement below that is true.

.... 1. Summaries are short statements of important facts.
.... 2. Cramming is a good way to study for a test.
.... 3. A schedule helps you organize your time.
.... 4. To find a specific fact, you should skim material.
.... 5. When you scan, you do not read every word.
.... 6. Study-reading is slow and careful reading.
.... 7. You should skim at your normal reading rate.
.... 8. It is always important to read everything carefully.
.... 9. When you skim, you lose understanding.
.... 10. A weekly schedule helps you plan long-range assignments.

B. Study-read the next passage. Then put an X in the box beside the correct ending to each statement that follows. There may be more than one correct ending.

If you could cut a wedge out of the Earth you would find a very dense, heavy **inner core**. As the Earth was forming, heavy materials such as iron and nickel formed this solid core. Around the inner core is the **outer core**, which is made of hot, liquid materials. The diameter of the whole core is about 2,200 miles. The next layer, the **mantle**, is about 1,800 miles thick. It consists of heavy rocks. The **crust**, or outermost layer, is formed from lighter materials, mostly granite and basalt. It varies from 5 to 20 miles in thickness.

1. The Earth's crust is
   □ a. the outermost layer.
   □ b. about 4000 miles thick.
   □ c. mostly granite.

2. The Earth is made up of
   □ a. four different layers.
   □ b. mostly hot, liquid rock.
   □ c. mostly iron and nickel.

3. The whole core is
   □ a. made up of the outer and the inner core.
   □ b. hot and liquid.
   □ c. 2,200 miles in diameter.

4. The Earth's mantle is
   □ a. thicker than the crust.
   □ b. heavy rocks.
   □ c. 1800 miles thick.

Developing Literary Skills

Distinguishing between Fiction and Nonfiction

Can you tell whether a book is fiction or nonfiction? Fiction, you recall, is the product of an author's imagination. It deals with people and events that are made up. Novels and short stories, for example, are fiction.

Nonfiction, on the other hand, deals with real people and events. Books about art or history are nonfiction. So is a **biography**, which is a story about a real person.

Sometimes it is easy to tell the difference between fiction and nonfiction. If the book is from the library, you can tell by looking at the **spine**, or back of the book. In some libraries, books are marked with an *F* for fiction. In others, they may be marked according to the type of fiction story they are—*M*, for mystery, say, or *W* for western. Nonfiction books have either a number or a *B* for biography. And sometimes biographies are marked by both a number and the letter *B*.

If the book is not a library book, you might be able to tell whether it is fiction from the title. Read the two titles below, for instance.

All About Flowering Plants

Tall Tales of the Old West

The first book is, of course, nonfiction. It is a book about plants. Since tall tales are made up, you know that the second book is fiction.

Sometimes a title includes a **subtitle** that explains what the book is about. Read the title below.

DOCTOR J
A Biography of Julius Erving

The subtitle explains that the book is nonfiction.

Some titles, though, are not so obvious. *Have Space Suit—Will Travel* could be either fiction or nonfiction. Is it the story of a real astronaut or is it made up? You would have to read some of the book to find out. (By the way, it is a novel.)

Often there is a brief report of the book on the paper cover, or jacket, or on the back cover. Sometimes quotes from people who have read the book are included, too. Reading them will usually tell you whether a book is fiction or nonfiction.

Now answer these questions about what you have just read. Then check them against the answer key on page 206.

1. What is the difference between fiction and nonfiction?

....

....

....

2. How can you tell whether a library book is fiction?

....

3. How does the library indicate a nonfiction book?

....

4. Write an *F* beside the titles below that are most likely fiction.

.... *Great Latin Sports Figures*

.... *The Frog Prince*

.... *The Story of Corn*

.... *Women in Sports: Tennis*

.... *Vietnamese Legends*

.... *Hobbies*

Reading a Work of Fiction

Books of fiction are fun to read. The story is often so interesting that you read quickly to find out what happens. But you don't want to read so fast that you miss important clues about what may happen next. You will enjoy a story more if you think about what you are reading.

As you read, pay attention to the author's choice of words. Listen to the sound of the words. Try to picture in your mind what the author is describing. Imagine yourself in the scene. Imagine that you are experiencing it through your senses—sight, hearing, taste, smell and touch. That will make the words come to life.

From time to time during your reading, stop and think about what you have read up to that point. Ask yourself questions such as the following:

- Are the events in the story true-to-life?
  Could they have really happened?

- If I were part of the story, how would I act?

- Do I like the characters in the book?
  Why or why not?
  Do they behave like anyone I know?

- Is the ending of the story a good one?
  Would I have ended it differently?

- Why did the author write the book?

- Would I recommend the book?
  Why or why not?

When you have finished the book, discuss it with other people who like to read.

If you liked it, try to convince them to read the book. If you did not like it, explain why. Briefly describe the plot, but don't give away the ending. Give your opinions about the characters, events and ideas. Use the questions you asked yourself as a guide in presenting those opinions.

A Write the answers to the questions below on the blank lines.

1. List three fiction books you have read.

....

....

....

2. Briefly describe the plot in one of the books.

....

....

....

....

....

....

3. In two or three sentences, explain why you did or did not like the book.

....

....

....

....

▶

B Read the following passage. Then answer the questions.

I couldn't believe my eyes. The spaceship came down through the night sky like a giant saucer. It flashed like a neon sign, in red, blue, green and yellow lights. My heart beat wildly. I was frightened, yes. But I was also excited. Wait until I tell the guys about this, I thought.

1. Do you think the event described in the passage could have really happened? Why or why not?

....

....

2. Picture the spaceship described in the passage. What does it look like?

....

....

3. Imagine yourself in the scene. Describe something about the spaceship not mentioned in the passage.

....

....

4. If you were part of the story, how would you act when you saw the spaceship?

....

....

5. Would you want to tell others about it? Why or why not?

....

....

Reading a Nonfiction Book

Reading a nonfiction book is different from reading a work of fiction. You will probably want to read more slowly, since it will contain much new information. You may want to take brief notes as you read.

Before you even begin reading, you should ask some questions. Who is the author? Is he or she an expert in the field? When was the book published? Is it up-to-date? If the book is not current, some events that would cause the information to be out-of-date may have occurred.

As with fiction reading, you will want to stop from time to time to think about the content. Is everything explained clearly? Does the author bring the subject to life? Is the book well illustrated? Does the book make you want to read more about the subject?

If the book is a biography, there are other questions you should ask. Did the author know the person personally? Did the author do a lot of research before writing the book? Is the book a true picture of the person, or is it one sided? Also, there are questions you can ask about the person whose biography it is. For instance, is the person famous or successful? What special qualities does the person have? Were his or her achievements the result of luck or hard work?

Asking those kinds of questions about a nonfiction book will help you get much more enjoyment from what you read.

☐ Read the questions that follow. Then write your answers on the blank lines.

1. Why is the publication date of a nonfiction book important?

....

....

2. Is it important for an author to be an expert on the book's subject? Why or why not?

....

....

▶

3. List three nonfiction books you have read recently.

....

....

....

4. In three or four sentences, explain why you liked one of the books. Use the questions in the lesson as a guide.

....

....

....

....

....

....

....

....

....

5. Why should an author do research before writing a biography?

....

....

6. Name three people you think would make good subjects for a biography.

....

....

....

7. Write three or four sentences about one of those people.

....

....

....

....

....

....

....

....

Recognizing Characters in Fiction

As you know, many stories are fiction, which means the characters in them are not real, they are made up. Made-up characters can *seem* like real people, though, as the following passage shows.

> When Laura saw Kitty Hawk for the first time, she felt very lonely. To her it was the end of the world.
>
> Her Uncle Henry sensed his niece's gloom and broke into her thoughts.
>
> "Don't worry, honey," he said. "There's lots to do here, you'll see. Looks kind of miserable now, but when it's clear and the ocean's calmer, you'll think you're in heaven."

Even when characters are not people, they can be made to seem real. Animals, as well as people, are often characters in stories. Notice how a dragon can be made to seem like a human.

> Great-aunt Pippa stared at the dragon. "You are not having Frederick, nor me, for your dinner," she said. "If you take one bite, one tiny chew or gnaw of my nephew, I'll destroy you."
>
> "Ha!" said the dragon. "If you mess around with me, old woman, I'll breathe my deadly flames on you and toast you."

From "Great-aunt Pippa's Pepperoni Pizza," by Lee Bennett Hopkins

Characters can even be things, like the sun, the rain, the wind or a river. In the next passage the main character is a river that is out of control. Yet the river seems real—it is a strong character.

> The river surged wildly. Its roar echoed down the valley, sounding like a scornful, shouted threat. It searched the banks with angry waves, eager to seize anyone or anything unlucky enough to be in its path. Bent on total destruction, the river plunged toward the village, where the people were scattering before its fury.

Complete each sentence in your own words. Check your answers against the key on page 206.

1. Because stories are fiction, the characters in them are

....

2. Characters do not have to be people; they can also be

.... or ....

3. Even when characters are not people, they can be made to

....

What Makes a Character?

Whoever acts or speaks in a story, a play or a novel is a character. As you have seen, characters can be people, animals or even things.

Not all characters in a story are important. We may not learn the names of some characters. Others may be mentioned only in passing. But there will always be at least one or two whom we will get to know very well. They will be the characters who are fully developed. We may like them or we may not. That is not important. What is important is that the writer will make these characters seem real. Often they are as real as people we know.

Writers develop their characters in many ways. One way is by describing a character's appearance. What do you learn from the description that follows?

> Rosa just knew it was going to be a great day. It was sunny and warm, an early spring morning. She had on her all-time favorite baggy sweater, and her sneakers, which made her feel like running to the bus stop instead of walking. She hummed along with the music that drifted out of every apartment on the block. It seemed that every kid listened to the same radio station. She began to walk a little faster, and her dark ponytail bounced up and down. Suddenly a smile burst across her face, causing her blue eyes to flash. "I can't wait to tell Ginger," Rosa said to herself as she broke into a jog, "she'll just love it!" Then she ran the last block to the bus stop, smiling all the way.

This description tells us that the character is feeling quite happy, and has some surprise to spring on her friend Ginger. We also get the idea that Rosa and Ginger are teenage schoolgirls. What can Rosa's surprise be? We don't know, and that makes us all the more curious to find out.

Another way writers develop characters is through the person's actions. What do you learn about Eric from the way he acts in the following passage?

Eric's arms hung limply by his sides. He stared, head down, at his shoes. Then the shrill blast of a whistle awakened him. With a grunt, Eric lifted his head high and walked back to the huddle. By the time he reached his teammates, his mind was made up. There was no time for fretting over past mistakes. He was eager to run the play again, and this time he planned to get it right.

Here we learn that Eric is a proud young man who does not like to make a fool of himself. He is also determined to become a better player. He learns from his mistakes and tries not to spend time feeling sorry for himself. In short, Eric sounds like the kind of person we'd like to get to know better.

☐ What can you learn about characters through description and through their actions? Read each paragraph carefully. Then answer the questions by putting an **X** in the box beside the letter of the answer that best completes each sentence.

A hundred and more years ago, Rip Van Winkle lived in a small village in New York. Rip was a simple, good-natured fellow, but he was lazy. Indeed, he would work harder at getting out of work than he would have worked at the job itself! Still, Rip was liked by everyone. Perhaps that was because he was kind and generous. Children especially would shout with joy whenever they saw him. For Rip made them toys, taught them to fly kites and shoot marbles, and told them wonderful stories of ghosts and witches and Indians.

1. In this passage you learn about Rip mostly through
   ☐ a. a description of what he was like.
   ☐ b. what Rip says.
   ☐ c. what others say about him.

▶

2. According to this passage, Rip's main fault is that he is
   - ☐ a. too proud.
   - ☐ b. a generous person.
   - ☐ c. lazy.

3. In the passage, the writer
   - ☐ a. makes fun of Rip.
   - ☐ b. points out that Rip is not well liked.
   - ☐ c. shows that he likes Rip.

Hannah gulped her glass of milk, snatched the books from the table, and dashed out of the cafeteria. A brief look at her watch told her she'd really better get moving, and she broke into an even faster run. Hannah flew up the stairs, turned left, and ran pell-mell down the hall, scattering students as she went. At last she burst through the door and sank into her seat, just as the bell went off. Hannah's record of never being late for class stood unbroken.

1. In this passage we learn about Hannah mostly through
   - ☐ a. her actions.
   - ☐ b. the way she talks.
   - ☐ c. how she looks.

2. You could say that Hannah is
   - ☐ a. foolish and frightened.
   - ☐ b. responsible but likes to put things off until the last moment.
   - ☐ c. lonely and unhappy.

3. It is important to Hannah that she
   - ☐ a. has a lot of friends in school.
   - ☐ b. can eat lunch faster than anyone else.
   - ☐ c. is never late to class.

Learning More about Characters

You have just learned that writers can develop characters by describing their appearance and their actions. There are also two other ways writers can develop characters. One way is by telling what the person says and thinks. What do you learn about the speaker in the following passage?

> The sea was quiet there. There was no sound of surf, and the moon shone brightly. I thought that I had never seen a place so empty and unfit to live in, but it was dry land, at long last. When I reached shallow water, I stood up and began to wade ashore. I couldn't tell whether I was more tired or more grateful that I was saved.

The speaker seems to be someone who was shipwrecked. Nearly lost at sea, he or she has reached land once more, and is tired but happy.

A fourth way writers develop characters is through what others say and think about them. Although Edith is not present during the following dialogue, we still learn about the kind of person she is.

> "Why don't you like Edith?" I asked.
> "Why don't I? I'll tell you," Nanny answered quickly.
> "She talks without thinking what it is she is saying. And that can hurt a person, you know. My mother used to tell me, 'Nanny, always taste the words before you let them slip off your tongue. If they taste the slightest bit sour to you, just think how someone else will take them.'"

From that dialogue we learn that Edith is guilty of speaking without thinking of the feelings of others. ▶

☐ What can you learn about characters through what they say and think, or through what others say and think about them? Read each passage carefully. Then answer the questions by putting an **X** in the box beside the letter of the answer that best completes each sentence.

It took a while, but I finally found the old man. He was sitting in front of an abandoned shack.

"What do you have to eat?" I asked.

"Some greens and 'possum. Do you want some?" he said.

"No, I ate at home," I said. "Let me make a fire for you."

"I'll eat later, Judd," the old man said. "For now, let's you and me just enjoy the sun."

I sighed and eased myself onto a log next to him. There were no greens and 'possum, I knew. And I also knew the old man was too proud to tell me that.

1. In this passage we learn about Judd mostly from
   ☐ a. what he says and thinks about himself and the old man.
   ☐ b. what the old man says about him.
   ☐ c. description.

2. We learn about the old man mostly through
   ☐ a. what he says and thinks about himself.
   ☐ b. what Judd says and thinks about him.
   ☐ c. what he does.

3. Having read the passage, it is fair to say that Judd
   ☐ a. thinks the old man is foolish.
   ☐ b. is sorry he found the old man.
   ☐ c. is concerned about the old man.

"Is that you, Juddy? Did you find him?"

"Yes, Mom, I found him," Judd answered as he entered the kitchen. "He was sitting on a log outside the abandoned shack down by the creek, just soaking up the sun."

"And he's . . . he's all right?" Judd's mother seemed almost afraid to ask.

"Yes, Mom, he's OK. But I don't think he's eaten anything in a couple of days."

"Well, then, we'll just fix him a nice hot meal and you can take it to him."

"He won't take it, Mom, I keep telling you. The old man wants to do it on his own, or he won't do it at all."

1. In this passage we learn about the old man mostly by
   □ a. his actions.
   □ b. description.
   □ c. what others say and think about him.

2. It seems that
   □ a. both Judd and his mother are afraid of the old man.
   □ b. Judd understands the old man a little better than his mother does.
   □ c. to Judd's mother, the old man is just another hungry wanderer.

3. Having read the passage, you could fairly say that the old man is
   □ a. sickly and lost.
   □ b. afraid and lonely.
   □ c. proud and stubborn.

Conflict and Plot Development

Characters make up one key element of a story. Two other key parts are the **plot** and the **conflict**.

The plot is made up of all the things that happen in the story. The events are arranged in an order that will hold the reader's interest. After all, if you can predict a story's ending long before you get there, you are not likely to want to go on reading.

Events in a story must follow one another in a way that makes sense. Of course, it's nice to have some surprises, but the surprises must be reasonable. First, the writer should leave clues about what is going to happen. And whatever events the character is involved in must seem right for that kind of person. To have a ten-year-old boy land a crippled airliner safely, for instance, would not be reasonable. But what if one of the passengers on the airliner happened to be a pilot? If that person took over the controls, the reader could say, "Yes, that might happen."

A plot must also have some kind of conflict. The conflict is the problem that will be settled before it ends.

In some stories the conflict has two people in a struggle against each other. It could be a story about two people trying out for the same part in a school play, for instance. In the end, only one of the two people will win the part.

In other stories a character may be in conflict with himself or herself. Have you ever been afraid to do something? Maybe you had to go to a new school and you were afraid on the first day, but you forced yourself to go anyway. That would be a struggle, or conflict, with yourself.

A conflict can also involve a person and nature. We've all read stories in which a person gets caught in a bad storm. Will he or she live through the storm? That is a conflict of character with nature.

Complete each sentence in your own words. Check your answers against the key on page 206.

1. The plot is made up of the ....
   in a story.

2. The action in a story is always arranged in some kind of

   ....

3. A good writer will leave .... about how
   how the story will end.

4. In a story, conflict is ....

   ....

5. Three kinds of conflict are .... against

   .... , ... against

   .... and ....

   against ....

Learning the Stages in Plot Development

The events in a story make up the plot. The author tries to arrange the events in a way that will catch—and hold—your interest. A typical story plot has a beginning, a middle, and an end. Certain things happen in each of those parts.

Introduction. The beginning is called the introduction. There you will meet the characters. You will find out who the main character is, and which characters will play supporting roles.

In the introduction you will also learn about the **setting**—where and when the story takes place. Is the setting familiar to you, or is it some wild and strange place? Does the story take place in the past, the present, or the future?

Early in the story you will also discover the **conflict**, or problem. Every story will have some kind of conflict. Of course, the conflict will involve the characters.

Middle. The middle of the story is often called the body. It is in the body that the plot unfolds. Somewhere in this part of the story you might begin to see how the conflict could be solved. That point in the story is called the **turning point**.

Suppose, for example, that Jane agrees to a tennis match with her friend Bart. She will never beat him, Jane thinks, because he plays so well. But as she gets into the match, Jane learns that she can keep up with Bart. That would be the turning point. Jane feels that she just might be able to win the match after all!

End. By the time you reach the ending, or **conclusion**, the conflict will be solved. In the tennis example, Jane might have overcome her lack of confidence and won the match.

Of course, in all stories the solution may not be a happy one. Even the main character can lose the struggle. The important thing is that the ending is the right one for the story. The turning point has given us a clue as to how the story will end. If the ending doesn't fit that clue, we are disappointed. Indeed, a wrong ending can spoil an otherwise enjoyable story.

A The list that follows breaks down a story into the four stages of plot development. Before each statement, write the stage it represents: *introduction, conflict, turning point* or *conclusion.*

.... 1. Fred proves to himself that he is as able a camper as his friend Andy.

.... 2. Night falls, and Fred begins to see that camping is not as bad as he had imagined.

.... 3. Although he is frightened by the idea of camping in the woods overnight, Fred agrees to go with Andy.

.... 4. Fred's friend Andy asks him to go camping over the weekend.

B Read the following plot summary carefully. Then write the events that belong in each stage of the plot development.

More than anything, Terry wants to have her own newspaper route. But Terry's parents don't think that is the kind of part-time job a young girl should have. They try to persuade her to take a baby-sitting course at the local Red Cross chapter. Terry is not happy with that suggestion. She arranges for her parents to talk with the person who oversees the newspaper carriers. Ms. Calabrese tells them of several young girls who are already carriers. Persuaded by what they hear, Terry's parents allow Terry to take on her own route.

1. Introduction ....

....

2. Conflict ....

....

3. Turning Point ....

....

....

4. Conclusion ....

....

Recognizing Kinds of Conflict

Conflict is the most important element in any story. In fact, you could say that without conflict there is no story.

Conflict involves a struggle. The struggle may occur between one person and another, or between a person and nature. Conflict can also occur within a person.

On page 175 you saw that Fred was not happy about going camping. He was afraid to stay in the woods all night. What's more, he probably did not want to admit to anyone that he was afraid. In that story, Fred's real conflict is with himself. He has to prove to himself that he can overcome his fear.

Suppose, though, that Fred likes camping as much as his friend Andy does. And while they are enjoying themselves in the woods, a flash flood causes the river to overflow its banks. That conflict would pit Fred and Andy against the river. It would be a conflict with nature.

What kind of conflict does the passage below reveal?

"Jesse . . . Jesse Lynch!" Mr. Fontaine's voice cut through the fog. Jesse was awakened from his dream. He stood up quickly, ignoring the giggles of his classmates.

"Jesse," Mr. Fontaine went on, "are you going to run for this class's seat on the Student Council? I have to have your name now if you're going to run."

Jesse knew the answer to that question all right. "Yes, sir, I sure am," he said.

Jesse couldn't wait to run against Luis Estrada, his rival. This time I'll beat him, he thought.

It is clear that the conflict here is between two people, Jesse and Luis.

There will be some kind of conflict in every story you read. And it will show up early, often just after you meet the characters and learn what the setting is. Make certain that you understand the conflict before you read on. The whole plot revolves around how that conflict will be solved. ▶

☐ On the blank lines, write the kind of conflict each passage shows. Choose from these kinds of conflict: (1) one person against himself or herself, (2) one person against nature, (3) one person against another.

"Well," the evil Captain Zook said, "we finally have you, Jason. And I daresay this time you'll not escape my clutches. I have sworn that you will live out your few remaining days here on the planet Kozar."

Jason's answer was as sharp and as cold as the look in his eyes. "I wouldn't bet my last spaceship on that, Zook."

....

Christie Weaver trudged out to the waiting airplane, fussing with her parachute as she went. Her ashen face and faraway look told the story. She was scared . . . no, terrified was more to the point.

"Why am I doing this?" Christie murmured to herself. "I hate airplanes and I get sick just thinking about heights. Yet here I am about to jump out of an airplane at eight thousand feet. Sometimes I just don't understand myself."

....

For years the North Atlantic Ocean had been considered dangerous. Indeed, it had claimed the lives of countless sea voyagers. And the day that sixteen-year-old Stenger Veendam set out from Holland in his tiny sailboat, that danger played heavily on his mind. Still he was eager to be off, eager to challenge the sullen gray sea. "This will be quite a voyage," he said to himself. "My best against the ocean's best. What could be more exciting?"

....

Mr. Brown squirmed nervously in his chair. He felt hot and sweaty, and his shirt collar was nearly choking him. He peered out at the people gathered together in the assembly hall. From his spot on the stage, they all looked alike. The thought of standing up in front of them to make a speech scared him silly. "I hate speaking to large groups," he muttered to himself, "why on earth did I ever agree to do this?" Then he heard his name; the master of ceremonies was introducing him to the crowd. He took three deep breaths and forced himself to smile. But the smile couldn't hide the fear in his eyes.

■

Setting and Mood in Fiction

On page 174 you learned that the setting of a story tells when and where the events take place. You also learned that the setting is described in the introduction of the story.

In some stories the setting may seem as real, perhaps, as a place you know.

> On every holiday, lovely cooking smells took over completely. In the cupboard were stacked newly baked delicacies such as sweet-potato pies, pecan pies and rich cakes. A grand turkey roasted slowly in the giant stove that took up a good bit of our kitchen. Nearby, mother busily kneaded bread. For his part, father prepared the several kinds of vegetables that would add to our dinner.

In other stories the setting might be a strange, unrealistic place, a product of the writer's imagination.

> I had no idea where I was. I had awakened from a dreamless sleep only to feel as if I were in the middle of a nightmare. I took off running across a vast, smooth lawn. Ahead of me I could see an oak tree that looked as if it had been hit by lightning. Only the trunk remained, splintered and evil looking. As I neared the tree a misshapen cloud crossed in front of the pale moon. Suddenly there was no light at all, and I stood still, waiting, in the darkness. When the moonlight returned, the tree was gone. The lawn, its dewy grass glittering softly in the dim moonlight, stretched out endlessly. Where was the oak tree? Where was I?

A setting can be realistic, as the first description is, or it can be strange and unrealistic, as the second description shows. And a story can be set in the past, the present or the future. The following passage is a good example of a story set in the future.

New Austin, that's our home. It's one of the colonies in space between Earth and Venus. Charlie, my kid brother, and I want to move to the new colony near Pluto in the worst way. But Mom and Dad won't hear of it.

"New Austin is our home," they say. "You kids were born here. We were born here. And Gramps and Grammy were born here. We're not leaving."

Complete each sentence in your own words. Check your answers against the key on page 206.

1. A setting tells ....

....

2. A setting is described in the ....
of a story.

3. The events in a story can take place in the .... ,

in the .... or in the ....

4. A setting may be .... , or it may be

....

Learning How the Setting Affects Characters

Where we live is our setting. It affects the way we live, act and think. For example, people who live in Florida are not likely to spend much time ice-skating or snow skiing. Those who live in Idaho may never get to swim in an ocean.

People in stories are also affected by their settings. Read the following story setting. How is Angela affected by it?

> Angela allowed herself a smile. She had fought with her parents about moving west. The sounds and sights of a great city were all she had known. And here she was in a corral astride her very own pony. She could hardly believe her good fortune. Her pony, Ginger, seemed to sense that this new rider and she would soon be friends. So she stood patiently, waiting for the gentle prod from Angela's boots that would tell her, "Angela wants us to ride off together!"

Clearly, Angela feels good about her setting. She likes where she lives. She likes her pony, Ginger. We look forward to good times for the both of them.

Now think about how the setting might affect the character in the next passage.

> The room I awoke in was on an upper floor. The one window looked out on an alley. A ledge three feet wide offered a walkway to a fire escape near the corner of the building. I stepped quickly to the window, my only chance of escape. Ever so carefully, I began to raise it. I knew that if any part of the frame snapped or the hinge creaked, I was a dead man. Ivan, who was standing guard outside my door, would surely hear it. And three of my companions were already victims of his murderous temper. I had no wish to become the fourth.

Here the character is not happy at all. Indeed, his life is in danger. And that fact affects his every move. As readers we share the feeling of danger and long to find out if he is able to escape.

☐ Read the following story settings carefully. Then put an **X** beside the answer that best completes each sentence.

They made their first trip to Oak Island twenty years ago. Oak Island was then a pleasant place. There were thick stands of evergreens and wild apple trees. Even a few of the red oaks that gave the island its name remained.

Here and there were lush raspberry fields and bushes laden with plump blueberries. Birds sang. Rabbits bounded through the underbrush. In short, Oak Island seemed no different from any of the 350 other islands in the same bay. But it was different. They soon found out just how different it was!

1. The story takes place
   ☐ a. in the past.
   ☐ b. in the present.
   ☐ c. in the future.

2. The setting is
   ☐ a. a lonely wilderness.
   ☐ b. a dangerous place.
   ☐ c. a pleasant little island.

3. The setting tells us that the speaker is likely to
   ☐ a. lose his life.
   ☐ b. uncover a buried treasure.
   ☐ c. discover some new and interesting things.

▶

The pirates' main base for their smuggling lay in the swampy bayous south of New Orleans. There, in an area called Baratavia, as many as one thousand people lived. There were single people and there were families. There were privateers and there were pirates. Still, most of the Baratavians lived quiet lives. They earned their living by fishing and trapping—and by smuggling. Most of those who were outlaws did not bother their neighbors. Those who did were dealt with quickly. Baratavians had their own code of justice. And the swamps had a way of keeping secrets.

1. The story takes place in
   ☐ a. the past.
   ☐ b. the present.
   ☐ c. the future.

2. Life in the swamps of Baratavia was
   ☐ a. difficult and unhappy.
   ☐ b. disappointing and scary.
   ☐ c. quiet, and at times dangerous.

3. Because of the setting, people who lived in Baratavia tended to
   ☐ a. be friendly and outgoing.
   ☐ b. keep to themselves.
   ☐ c. be concerned about what their neighbors did.

Learning about Mood in a Story

Everyone experiences different moods, or feelings, at different times. We laugh when we're happy and feel grouchy when we're in a bad mood.

Stories have moods as well. A funny story will put us in a happy mood. A story with an unhappy ending may leave us sad and quiet. Ghost stories are scary, and adventure stories leave us nervous, even breathless.

Authors are careful to create a single mood in each story they write. They help create the mood through the story setting. What mood does the following setting suggest to you?

> Storm clouds rushed in from the east. About 3 P.M. the sky grew dark and rain began to pelt down in short but violent bursts. All this time the wind was blowing harder and harder. People looked on in astonishment as the ocean rose higher and higher, until it dashed freely over the seawall.

That setting makes us glad we are not there. A mood of uneasiness and danger is building. If the storm continues, the mood may become one of horror.

Now look at another story setting to experience a different kind of mood.

> It must have been close to midnight when I awoke. I lay snuggled in my bed, warm and comfortable under heaps of quilts. Outside my window moonbeams painted a silver path across the sea. And the surf murmured a soft greeting to the beach every few seconds.

Here is a setting that puts us in a warm and pleasant mood. We'd like to be the person in that bed, who seems so happy. Words like *snuggled*, *warm*, *comfortable*, and *murmur* help to build this nice mood.

▶

☐ Read each story setting carefully. Then put an **X** in the box beside the answer that best completes each sentence.

John trudged along the furrows, his eyes staring dully at the ground, his numb hands wrapped around the reins. Ahead of him in the fading light, Ezra, the family's mule, strained under the weight of the plow. Ezra was ready to quit. He wanted the warmth of the barn. John could sense that. And in truth, John was ready too. But his father would hear nothing of quitting, John knew. The land had to be made ready for planting.

The mood of this passage is one of
☐ a. hatred of work.
☐ b. defeat and anger.
☐ c. fatigue mixed with a sense of purpose.

When early November came, the pond froze over. It was then that the mother beaver, her mate and their four youngsters took to their lodge under the ice. They lived there for five months. They had aspen tree branches for food, and the thick walls of the lodge protected them from their enemies and the winter storms. It was a warm, pleasant existence. And now, with nice weather soon to come, they began to prepare for another summer on the pond.

The mood of this passage is one of
☐ a. joy.
☐ b. security.
☐ c. gloom.

That day in July was hot—burning hot. Nonetheless, 35,000 people stood on the edges of a chasm that dropped 700 feet straight down. On the far side a man carefully checked the long thin wire that was anchored on both sides of the abyss. He was resplendent in maroon and gold tights. He stepped nimbly onto the wire. An assistant passed him a balancing pole. The tightrope walker made his way, very slowly, out over the chasm. Halfway across, he paused on the wire. No one uttered a word. Indeed, few people even breathed. Would the man go on across, or would he quit? And if he continued, would he make the perilous trip, or would he fall?

The mood of this passage is one of
☐ a. excitement and suspense.
☐ b. surprise and joy.
☐ c. delight and hope.

■

Rhyme and Rhythm in Poetry

Rhyme and rhythm are a regular part of our lives. They are used commonly in our language as well. We met rhyme, which is a matching final sound in words, when we were very young. Do you know any rhyming games? Here is one used in choosing up sides:

> Engine, engine, number nine,
> Going down Chicago line,
> If the train should jump the track,
> Do you want your money back?
> Yes.
> No.
> Maybe so.

Did you notice the rhyming words? They are *nine* with *line*, *track* with *back*, and *no* with *so*.

Perhaps you first learned your numbers with rhymes like this:

> One, two,
> Buckle my shoe.
> Three, four,
> Shut the door . . . .

Even adults use rhymes to remember useful things:

> Rain before seven;
> Clear by eleven.

> Thirty days hath September,
> April, June, and November . . . .

Rhythm, too, is all around us. It is in nature. Rhythm can be seen in the regular changing of night to day, and it can be seen in the rising and falling of the tides. Rhythm occurs

naturally in our language, too. We accent, or stress, one syllable above the others in many words.

a • BOVE   ad • MIS • sion   AC • cent

And rhythm is the heartbeat of poetry. Rhythm is the order of sounds that makes you want to clap your hands or tap your feet. Read the following lines of poetry to yourself softly. You should hear a strong, regular rhythm, or beat, in the verse.

Sing a song of seasons!
  Something bright in all!
Flowers in the summer,
  Fires in the fall!

Complete each sentence in your own words. Check your answers against the key on page 206.

1. Rhyme is ....

....

2. In poetry, rhythm is ....

....

3. Two examples of rhythm in nature are ....

.... and ....

4. Two words that rhyme are ....

and ....

Recognizing Rhymes and Rhyme Schemes

Many poems use rhyming words. Rhymes make poetry more musical, and they make learning the lines easier, as well. Rhymes, you will remember, are matching final sounds in words. Can you find the rhymes in these lines?

> Who has seen the wind?
>   Neither you nor I:
> But when the trees bow down their heads
>   The wind is passing by.

The rhyming words are *I* in the second line and *by* in the fourth line. Notice that the rhyming words come at the ends of those lines. Some poems have rhyming words in the same line. Here is one example.

> The stars never *rise*, but I feel the bright *eyes*

Now underline the rhyming words in these lines from a very old poem.

> I cannot eat but little meat
>   My stomache is not good . . .

Did you underline *eat* and *meat?* If so, you were right.

Remember then, when you read poems you can often expect to find words that rhyme with each other within one line, which is called **internal rhyme**, as well as at the ends of different lines. And if you decide to write your own poems, you can construct the rhymes in those ways.

When you read a poem, you may notice that the rhymes often follow a regular pattern, or **rhyme scheme**. Here is one popular kind of rhyme scheme:

> In winter I get up at night
> And dress by yellow candle light.
> In summer, quite the other way,
> I have to go to bed by day.

The first and second lines rhyme, and so do the third and fourth. You can show a rhyme scheme, which is the order of the rhymes in a poem, by assigning a letter of the alphabet to each rhyming sound. In the poem you just read, the rhyme scheme is *a a b b*. We assign the letter *a* to the sound at the end of the first line. Every other line that ends in that sound is also *a*. The second rhyming sound is called *b*, and so on. An ending sound that has no rhyme is called *x*.

What is the rhyme scheme in these lines?

> The moon comes every night to peep
> Through the window where I lie;
> But I pretend to be asleep
> And watch the moon go slowly by . . .
>
> From "The White Window," by James Stephens

Did you write *a b a b*? If so, you were right. The first and third lines rhyme, and the second and fourth lines rhyme. Look back at the first poem in this lesson (the one that begins "Who has seen the wind?"). The rhyme scheme for that poem would be written like this: *x a x a*. The first and third lines do not have any rhymes. The second line has the first rhyming sound, so it is *a*. It rhymes with the last line.

|A| Draw a circle around the words that have rhymes in the poems below. Then connect each pair of rhyming words with a line.

1. Darkness settles on roofs and walls,
   But the sea, the sea in the darkness calls;
   The gentle waves, with their soft, white hands,
   Erase the footprints in the sands,
     And the tide rises, the tide falls.

2. Does the road wind uphill all the way?
     Yes, to the very end.
   Will the day's journey take the whole long day?
     From morn to night, my friend.

▶

3. So here we have dawning
   Another blue day.
   Think, will you let it
   Slip uselessly away?

4. There was a young lady of Niger
   Who smiled as she rode on a tiger;
   They returned from the ride
   With the lady inside
   And the smile on the face of the tiger.

5. The dogs do bray, and the timbrels play;
   The spindle is now a-turning;
   The moon it is red, and the stars are fled,
   But the sky is all a-burning.

B Using letters of the alphabet, write the rhyme schemes of each of the above poems.

1. ....

2. ....

3. ....

4. ....

5. ....

■

Learning about Rhythm

Not all poems will have rhyming words, but all poems will have some kind of rhythm. You are familiar with rhythm in music—it is the regular, repeated sound that makes you want to clap your hands and tap your feet. In poetry, rhythm is made by the way the words in each line are pronounced.

Rhythm in a line of poetry, then, depends on which words are stressed, or emphasized, over others. Most poets choose words very carefully, and they use them in ways that lead you naturally to stress the ones they wish you to stress. Look at the following line of poetry, for instance. Read it softly to yourself. Do you feel the rhythm? Put accent marks (/) over the words you think should be stressed.

Whose woods these are I think I know

If you caught the rhythm of that line, you would have accented it like this:

Whose woóds these aŕe I thińk I knów

Did you also notice how regular the rhythm was in the line? Now try another line. It too has a regular rhythm, but that rhythm is different.

Tramp across the pasture

With the accented syllables, that line looks like this:

Trámp acróss the pásture

The lines below are examples of two other kinds of regular rhythm in poems.

Ońe more unfórtunate pérson like thése

For the moón never beáms without brińging me dreáms ▶

Of course, not all poems have such regular rhythm as those examples. The point to remember is that every poem will have *some* kind of rhythm. If you can recognize that rhythm, you will enjoy reading the poem more, and you will find that you have an easier time understanding what the poem is saying.

[A] Read the following lines from different poems softly to yourself, then put an accent mark (/) over each word or syllable that should be stressed.

1. How straight it flew, how long it flew

2. Then away bound for home, we did march on to Rome

3. Just for a ribbon of silver he sold us

4. I am the master of my fate,
   I am the captain of my soul

5. And the stars never rise but I see the bright eyes
   of my beautiful Annabel Lee

6. I meant to do my work today

[B] Do the same with the following lines of poetry—but notice that the rhythm is not always regular. It may change from one line to the next.

1. If a pig wore a wig,
   What could we say?
   Treat him as a gentleman,
   And say, "Good day."
   If his tail chanced to fail,
   What could we do?
   Send him to the tailor
   To get one new.

2. He clasps the crag with crooked hands;
   Close to the sun in lonely lands . . .

3. Hopping frog, hop here and be seen,
       I'll not pelt you with stick or stone;
   Your cap is laced and your coat is green;
       Goodbye, we'll let each other alone.   ■

Literary Skills Achievement Test

I. Fiction and Nonfiction

Put an **X** in the box beside the ending that best completes each statement below.

1. Fiction deals with made-up people and events, and nonfiction
   - ☐ a. is only about famous people.
   - ☐ b. deals with real people and events.
   - ☐ c. deals with real places, but made-up people.

2. Nonfiction library books are marked with
   - ☐ a. a number or a *B*.
   - ☐ b. the letters *NF*.
   - ☐ c. the word *nonfiction*.

3. The book *Six Fairy Tales* is probably
   - ☐ a. fiction.
   - ☐ b. nonfiction.
   - ☐ c. neither.

4. The book *Frontiers of Dance: The Life of Martha Graham* is probably classed as
   - ☐ a. history.
   - ☐ b. fiction.
   - ☐ c. biography.

5. When you read fiction, you should
   - ☐ a. imagine yourself in the scene.
   - ☐ b. look ahead to the ending.
   - ☐ c. read as quickly as possible.

6. When reading nonfiction, you should know
   - ☐ a. whether the author is an expert in his or her field.
   - ☐ b. where the author was born.
   - ☐ c. the age of the author.

7. If a nonfiction book was published a long time ago, it
   - ☐ a. is probably incorrect.
   - ☐ b. is not worth reading.
   - ☐ c. may have outdated information.

8. A biography is a book about a
   - ☐ a. person, by that person.
   - ☐ b. real person.
   - ☐ c. made-up person.

II. Recognizing Characters

Read the following description carefully. Then put an **X** in the box beside the answer that best completes each statement.

> "Now this is the life," I said to myself. I was deep in the woods . . . alone. And I'd stay at least a week. No people were around, just animals, which I could hear in the brush, and birds, which I could see. My friends have never been able to understand why I like the wilderness. Maybe they don't feel the need to get away every now and then. I do. And I like to match myself against nature.

1. The character shows himself to be
   - ☐ a. selfish and lonely.
   - ☐ b. independent and strong.
   - ☐ c. fearful and stubborn.

2. We learn about this character through
   - ☐ a. his own thoughts.
   - ☐ b. what others say about him.
   - ☐ c. the setting.

III. Learning about Plot and Conflict

A. Put an **X** in the box beside the answer that best completes each statement.

1. The one term that does *not* name a stage in plot development is
   ☐ a. conflict.
   ☐ b. turning point.
   ☐ c. mood.

2. The most important part of any story is the
   ☐ a. cast of characters.
   ☐ b. setting.
   ☐ c. conflict.

3. Another name for conflict is
   ☐ a. struggle.
   ☐ b. conclusion.
   ☐ c. introduction.

B. Read the following passages carefully. Then put an **X** in the box beside the answer that best completes the statement.

"No, Don," Marie stated firmly. "I don't want to go to a rock show—loud music hurts my ears."

"Come on, Marie," Don said, "I'll give you some earplugs. And you can wear earmuffs over those. You won't look *too* silly."

Marie pictured herself in earmuffs at a rock show. "No way," she muttered to herself, "I'm not going, and that's final."

"What did you say?" Don asked.

"I said I'm not going, and that's final."

Don, looking glum, gave up. He knew that Marie never budged once she made up her mind. He wouldn't be able to talk her into going no matter how hard he tried.

1. The passage is an example of conflict between
   ☐ a. a person and nature.
   ☐ b. a person and himself or herself.
   ☐ c. one person and another person.

2. What is the probable outcome of the conflict?
   ☐ a. Marie and Don will go to the rock show together.
   ☐ b. Marie will go to the rock show alone.
   ☐ c. Marie will not go to the rock show, and Don will go by himself.

3. What line in the passage best indicates the turning point?
   ☐ a. Don, looking glum, gave up.
   ☐ b. "No, Don," Marie stated firmly.
   ☐ c. Marie pictured herself in earmuffs at a rock show.

IV. Recognizing Setting and Mood

Put an **X** in the box beside the answer that best completes each statement.

1. The setting of a story
   ☐ a. is the same as the conclusion.
   ☐ b. tells when and where the events take place.
   ☐ c. usually is described in the turning point.

2. The setting of a story
   ☐ a. should have no effect on the characters.
   ☐ b. affects the way the characters act and think.
   ☐ c. depends on the conflict.

3. The mood of a story is created by the
   ☐ a. conflict.
   ☐ b. setting.
   ☐ c. conclusion.

V. Learning about Rhyme and Rhythm

A. Use this excerpt from Henry Wadsworth Longfellow's "My Lost Youth" to answer the questions that follow.

> Often I think of the beautiful town
>   That is seated by the sea;
> Often in thought go up and down
> The pleasant streets of that dear old town,
>   And my youth comes back to me.
>   And a verse of a Lapland song
>   Is haunting my memory still:
>   "A boy's will is the wind's will,
> And the thoughts of youth are long, long thoughts."

1. What is the rhythm of the first line of the poem? Put the accents over the proper syllables in that line, below.

   Often I think of the beautiful town

2. What is the rhyme scheme of the poem? Write the scheme on this line.

   ....

3. Which line in the poem uses internal rhyme, or rhymes in the same line? Write the line in this blank space and draw a circle around each of the words that rhyme.

   ....

B. Use this poem (which was written in 1773) to answer the questions that follow.

A Guinea-pig Song

There was a little guinea-pig,
Who, being little, was not big;
He always walked upon his feet,
And never fasted when he eat.

When from a place he run away,
He never at the place did stay;
And while he run, as I am told,
He ne'er stood still for young or old.

He often squeaked, and sometimes violent,
And when he squeaked he ne'er was silent.
Though ne'er instructed by a cat,
He knew a mouse was not a rat.

One day, as I am certified,
He took a whim and fairly died;
And as I am told by men of sense,
He never has been living since.

—Anonymous

1. What is the poem's rhyme scheme?

....

2. Put the accents over the words in the lines reproduced below.

When from a place he run away,
He never at the place did stay;

3. Does this poem use internal rhyme? ....